Introduction

During 2012 the conglomerate I was employed by was implementing a divestment strategy to maximise shareholder value, and the buyers for the division I worked in did not see a strategic fit for the business unit I was responsible for - it happens.

I started 2013 reflecting on what I wanted to do, would enjoy doing, and would enable me to pay the mortgage, feed my children and release more time to do 'other things' - you could say I had my covid lockdown moment earlier than most, when I chose to sacrifice salary for time.

"If I could secure 100 paid days without spending the other 265 days looking for them, then I'd be able to do other things".

Having worked in companies of all shapes, sectors, and sizes, with revenues of millions to billions, I can state that the challenges tended to be the same, just with a few more or a few less noughts attached.

How to improve the performance of your people, the profitability of your products and the productivity of your processes. In short, I'd been paid throughout my corporate career to improve business performance - from bars of soap to bars of gold.

By the end of that summer The Value Innovator, a *me-only-company* was registered and opened for business. Over those first 10 years, I completed hundreds of paid and unpaid mentoring sessions, facilitated boards, senior management teams and peer-to-peer groups. Worked with start-ups, scale-ups, plateaued and high growth companies; and wrote countless articles, presentations, courses, blogs and workshops on the challenges and opportunities facing owners, directors, and leaders of SMEs.

Value Warning: Please do not attempt to read this book from the first page to the last page as you would a novel, rather take one P at a time, 4 steps at a time.

1. Identify what's of benefit to you, your company, and your people.

2. Use the margin / back of the book space to jot down initial thoughts.

3. Decide on what offers the most immediate improvement potential.

4. Act swiftly to implement and complete each improvement before moving on to the next P.

To help context some of my comments and opinions over a decade that has witnessed the credit crunch fall-out, geopolitics, Brexit, a pandemic, recession, inflation, a cost-of-living crisis, and war in Europe; I have added the year each *chapter* was originally written; and throughout have done my best to attribute references and quotes.

What people say about Michael

"Michael is known for his leadership in team building and strategic positioning. He has a high industry profile and is well respected by customers and competitors."
Rich Powers, Divisional CEO Cookson Group plc.

"Michael is a conscientious and dynamic leader. He took time to understand the challenges, provided innovative solutions and actively sought out opportunities to make the project a success."
Victoria Waugh, Fairtrade Foundation

"Michael has been an excellent business mentor. He is non-judgemental and despite his obvious wealth of experience, was respectful of my small but growing business, and that was much appreciated. Thank you Michael I sincerely appreciate your time, guidance, and humour."
Jo Kenny, Curve Sales Solutions

"Thank you for being a most focussed and professional moderator, and doing an excellent job keeping us on track, whilst directing and helping us understand the priorities."
Gary Williams, Chairman Hatton Garden BID Development

"Your workshop was insightful, and your methods are so logical and understandable."
Sam Lloyd, FGA EG London

*"There are some people on this planet that I know can make a difference in how we think, how we act, and how we move forward in not only our actions but our attitude too.
One such person is Michael Donaldson."*
Sadie Skipworth, Social Media Specialist

"Michael's supportive management style was one of the key drivers in allowing myself, and my colleagues in Ireland to successfully achieve our strategic aims."
Ken O'Brien, MBA Business Operations Manager

Contents

Introduction

What people say about Michael

Part 1: People
1. What NO really means.	8
2. Key skills required for effective communication in a crisis.	10
3. Do you want great questions or great answers?	15
4. Life's more interesting when you listen.	18
5. We only see what we want to see.	20
6. Engage your customers by engaging your staff.	22
7. What's the purpose of a mind if you can't change it?	24
8. Good performers recognise the world's changing acquire new skills.	26
9. Careers and cocktails - now's the time.	28
10. A career choice requires courage and confidence.	30
11. Managers and Directors should act like Owners.	33
12. Are you a holiday wimp?	35
13. The skills for growth were they developed or axed in the recession?	37
14. Your business may have grown, but have you?	39
15. Would you follow your leadership style?	41
16. Which voice dominates your business?	45
17. Better boss better business.	48
18. Even those at the top need nourishment.	53
19. It's time to reset your Leadership compass.	56
20. Do your people know what good looks like?	58
21. If experience doesn't meet expectation you lose.	60
22. The male pale stale board.	64
23. I'm the monster my boss created.	66
24. Essential advice from non-essential business owners.	68
25. How putting people first improves profits.	70
26. How many game changers do you employ?	73

27. Are you too busy doing stuff?	75
28. The ideal employee and the C word.	78
29. This is the self-preservation society.	80
30. Don't go breaking my heart.	81
31. Happy or Content - asked the president.	83
32. Has the internet killed the sales professional?	85
33. Project success depends on your process jockey.	87
34. Are your Marketers' T shaped or I shaped?	90

Part 2: Product

35. How sustainable is your USP?	93
36. What makes your business so special?	95
37. Carpet	96
38. Great products or great marketing - which one matters the most?	97
39. Remember everyone is an expert in marketing.	98
40. Customer Shoes – walk in them to better your business.	100
41. Conditioner.	103
42. Demand for greater marketing ROI.	104
43. Performance or market Improvement where's your growth from?	107
44. Jewellery.	111
45. Ditch print at your own risk.	113
46. Trade Fairs - all marketing and no sales.	115
47. Strategy doesn't have to be complicated lessons from a car maker.	117
48. Appliances.	119

Part 3: Process

49. Tricky conversations made easier.	121
50. Managing motivational meetings.	123
51. When saying NO can enhance your brand reputation.	125
52. Slogans attract, stories engage, sales pay bills.	128
53. How do you connect with people's emotions in an advert?	130
54. Company centric processes cost you.	132
55. Is there a process for assessing company culture?	135

56. How to stop internal email undermining business growth.   137
57. Difficult conversations a necessity rarely a pleasure often avoided. 139
58. The good, the bad and the ugly redundancies.   141
59. Many appointments fail because of a poor interview /er.   144
60. 10 Reasons why appraisals fail.   149
61. Promotion should be a piece of pie.   151
62. Secrets of success and succession.   154
63. Seven questions every board needs to answer asap.   156
64. Acceptable is not acceptable.   162
65. How to navigate wage inflation.   166
66. Are you spending enough time on your business to deliver growth 170
67. How to realise data value from data usage.   172
68. Does your company have a growth culture?   176
69. We don't know what we don't know.   179
70. Do you run your business, or does it run you?   182
71. Cultural cows and cakes could close you.   184
72. Menopause needs men to implement the 'menostart'.   188
73. A goal without a plan is just a wish.   191
74. WeWork not as we used too - culture challenge.   195
75. Are you in control of your cyber creep?   199
76. Five step process to successful range management.   201
77. Whether it's big data or small data if you don't use it, it's just data.206
78. KPI's love them, loathe them, tips to help you use not abuse them.208
79. Have you reviewed your annual plan - as it could be out of date? 209
80. Marketing - only as good as your brief.   210
81. How to be found in a crowded market.   213
82. How to attract and retain new customers.   215
83. My 12 Leadership Lessons forged in recession, administration, and a world cup final.   220
84. Your People notes.   230
85. Your Product notes.   231
86. Your Process notes.   232

How to improve the performance of your PEOPLE

-1-
What NO really means
2015

New Parents often promise themselves never to use the word NO when speaking to their children, choosing instead to use alternate words, which is good in principle, develops language skills but exhausting and particularly irritating when they become "inbetweeners".

There was a time when Trainers would tell you that "if don't hear the word NO more than you hear the word Yes - you're not asking enough of your customers."

The word NO is probably one of the most over used words in the English language. It can be used as an Adverb, Adjective, Idiom, Noun, and Verb, it's even a chemical symbol; but it is universally regarded in the negative – as a REJECTION and no one likes to be rejected.

Yet it is vital in business that you understand what NO really means (in context) as it can be the difference between success and failure.

Let's ignore the obvious buyer seller interaction and consider a situation most of us can more easily relate to - trying to get someone to do something for you, whether that's in the office or the home!

Here are a few well-chosen words that may lie behind the next NO you hear:

- I'm too busy.
- It's not important enough to me.

- I'm alright doing what I'm doing.
- It's too complicated.
- I don't know you.
- I don't respect you.
- I don't trust you.
- I don't like you.
- I don't understand you.
- What's in it for me?
- It's beyond me.
- I'm afraid to let you down.
- I don't want to embarrass myself.
- I can't make that decision.
- I can't take that decision.

Once you understand what NO really means (and how best to respond to it) life gets easier and far more rewarding.

-2-
Key skills required for effective communication in a CRISIS
2020

The 3 key components to good communication are the message, the method, and the Messenger: most organisations focus on the first two and give little thought to the third by automatically defaulting to the person at the top of the organisation.

Over the years, across a variety of sectors, in a variety of situations including closures, acquisitions, administration, bird flu and a couple of military coups; I've been exposed to good communication, poor communication, sensitive communication and damaging communication – which was often down to the individual skills of the communicator than the content of the message, because the way you communicate is just as critical as having the right message.

The coronavirus pandemic has placed extraordinary demands on business leaders and their people. The sequence of events unfolding with overwhelming speed is generating a high degree of uncertainty, anxiety and in some cases fear. The first peak is believed to have passed (tbc) and the lockdown extended for a further 3 weeks; but we don't know how many lockdowns or peaks we may have to endure to defeat this terrible virus. We could still be social distancing in June and then again in the Autumn, we just don't know. The humanitarian toll in cases and deaths, closures and restrictions, salaries and shortages has unsettled many emotionally, physically, mentally, and spiritually.

In reality, we are dealing with two contagions; C19 and the emotions it generates – many of which are negative and every bit as contagious as the virus.

The majority of businesses I spoke to prior to the recent social distancing extension, had ticked all the functional boxes: they'd sent their HR letters, set up their WhatsApp groups, purchased zoom, circulated team brief schedules and delivered their maiden address to the staff. At the outset of a crisis, we often see leaders hitting the wrong notes, making Churchillian speeches, overconfident statements, and upbeat commitments to rally the "troops" and allay any fears, before the full facts are known - which can undermine their credibility as things unfold.

However, as we enter phase two (and future phases), communications will need to be more sensitive and less functional, as the mood of their staff changes.

The lack of testing and shortage of front line PPE have added to the general sense of a "lack of control" over what's happening, which has added to personal frustrations and negative emotions (despite the media's good news broadcasts) on everything from finances, to travel bans, food queues, closed high streets, vulnerable parents, home schooling and not being able to visit family and friends – all of which will increasing impact their staff emotionally, physically, mentally and spiritually.

A pre coronavirus survey by McKinsey shared specific examples of how people around the world have tended to cope during a crisis, in these very personal areas of their lives.

Emotional
A Mexican company vice president chooses to recharge by reaching out to friends regularly to send thanks and love.
A Swedish entrepreneur reviews an e-mail folder where she keeps compliments, thank-you notes, and warm greetings.

Physical
A Brazilian executive walks up a few flights of stairs quickly - more flights if she is agitated or upset - and then she slowly walks down, giving herself the time to reflect and come back to center.
An Italian senior manager has an afternoon coffee, walking to the lobby café instead of the coffee stand on his own floor.

Mental
When a US CEO needs to recharge his energy levels, he consciously seeks out conversations with employees, so he can learn something new.

Spiritual
A technology executive turns her chair to look out the window, meditating on nature and life in the form of the oak tree that fills her view. A UK Christian Director who talks to God throughout the day.

Responses will differ from one person to another, and what could be very emotional for one person may not be so for another, so whilst it's all relative try to remember that it's very real for the individual going through them. So, take time to see how your staff are being affected in particular ways, pay careful attention to how people are struggling and take corresponding measures to support them.

One helpful tool to help you recognise where your staff are, is the Kubler- Ross change curve which tracks the different phases people move through when coping with change, and signals what you need to do to get each individual along and back up the curve.

Watch and learn from others – Jeff Bezos' open coronavirus letter to his Amazon staff uses a simple but effective 5 step structure.
   1. Be truthful
   2. Express Gratitude
   3. Manage Expectations
   4. Address the Obvious
   5. Show your commitment

Working from home has also raised more than a few challenges, aside from the home schooling, lack of desk space, and 24/7 family life; I've noticed that people want to talk, and I mean talk about life in general (and then work) during the coronavirus which has challenged me to change my own approach. I have now started replying to texts and certain emails by calling people back, because I can, and it is good to talk.

But many of your employees may not be used to working from home and all of them are likely to have some concerns about their jobs, salary, and the company's future; as well as what is going on in their lives. Adapting your style to increase the intimacy of communications that replace the normal workplace face-to-face conversations will go a long way to offer them clarity and reassurance, as well as keeping them engaged with you, their work, and the company.

And 5 more tips from many to finish with:

1. Promote psychological SAFETY so people can openly discuss ideas, questions, and concerns without fear of repercussions. This allows the network of teams to make sense of the situation, and how to handle it through healthy debate.

2. Keeping the TONE of your communications in-line with your culture, values and employee value proposition will give a sense of authenticity and build a feeling of safety and trust.

3. Continually collect INFORMATION as the crisis unfolds and identify the potential impact on your people within your organisation - then update and consider its value in communicating.

4. Promote COMMUNITY involvement – which builds a sense of wellbeing whether that's local shopping support, contacting neighbours, offering the elderly contact, support those on the front line, produce or supply required products etc

5. Become more aware of YOURSELF what you are feeling at any given moment. Develop the ability to recognise your emotions, and the warning flags. Stay calm don't allow them to dictate your behaviour, and regardless of what's going on around you choose to focus on what you have the power to influence and ignore the other stuff - And if you can do all that, you'll certainly be a better person than me!

"People will forget what you said, they will forget what you did but people will never forget how YOU made them feel".
Maya Angelo

-3-
Do you want great questions or great answers?
2020

At first glance, coaching and mentoring may seem to be the same thing and are often transposed in our thinking as they are both techniques requiring similar skills to drive behavioural change, yet the process and the outcomes are quite different.

What is the difference between a coach and a mentor?
The International Coach Federation defines coaching as *"Partnering with clients in a thought-provoking and creative process that inspires them to maximise their personal and professional potential."*

The International Mentoring Group defines mentoring as, *"A process of direct transfer of experience and knowledge from one person to another."*

It might help to think of a mentor as an experienced and trusted advisor, with whom you have an enduring relationship based on confidentiality and respect, that enables you to tap into their experience and expertise when required. Think Obi Wan Kenobi and Luke Skywalker, Dumbledore and Harry Potter, Mr. Miyagi and Daniel LaRusso or for those who appreciate the beautiful game Joe Mercer and Malcolm Allison, Pep Guardiola and Mikel Arteta.

Now if you do not need *"a brain to pick, an ear to listen and a push in the right direction" (J.C.Crosby)* there's no need to read any further. However, if you would like some insight on when to use a mentor, the mindset of a mentee and how to get the most from a mentor continue reading.

I was informally mentored by Larry, an American colleague 15 years my senior and experienced in many things I had yet to experience. Through frequent meetings in various countries, at various events, we developed a mutual respect and trust. Which enabled me to reach out to him when faced with a significant downturn in UK demand which was threatening our factory and our employee livelihoods.

18 months on and I had stopped writing orders for 10s of thousands of units and had started writing orders for millions of units. I was no longer just selling to my regular UK customers, I was selling to new Chinese customers who in turn were selling to UK customers whose doors I'd been unable to open and to an entirely new market in the US.

When to use a mentor?
Most people don't ask for a mentor as they tend to be too involved in the day to day of the business or have a blind spot to the opportunities a mentor offers in terms of personal and professional development, or they may just be too embarrassed to ask for support and guidance.

The majority of people I have mentored have been introduced to me via a more senior person within their organisation, someone responsible for the future of the business, someone thinking about that individual's contribution, development and future role in the business.

Increasingly, I am being asked for advice and perspective on running and managing a board of directors or finding myself in conversation with business owners that know they need help but just *"don't know where to start".*

> *"Over the years, we've learnt that guidance and mentoring can help a business go from good, to the fastest growing company in the UK."*
> Gymshark X Innovation Birmingham Programme

What is required of the mentee?
I have learnt that the mindset of the mentee is critical - the trigger is recognising the need for support and that we cannot do everything on our own. The value comes from being receptive to advice and maintaining an open mind, no matter how improbable things may sound at times.

While many companies offer an internal mentor to support individuals identified as potential future leaders, it is common for mentees to work with mentors from outside their company or even industry sector, as it offers access to broader experience, new perspectives, and transferable insights – it also increases the reassurance of what's shared in the session stays in the session.

How to get the most from your mentor?
With a mentor you set the agenda and together you create the session in a way that works for you and helps you to build a better business. A good mentor not only brings business experience but life experience and a valuable perspective on wellbeing - 3 key ingredients for good Leadership.

At the start decide what assistance you need, what you want as your outcome and what are the ground rules. Process agreed, you will then need to engage with your mentor which may make demands on your EQ (emotional intelligence) as you establish a trust and respect for your mentor and open your heart as well as your mind to them, but that goes for any good relationship.

At first glance mentoring and coaching, may seem the same thing but the key difference is a coach has some great questions for your answers and a mentor has some great answers for your questions... all you have to do is ask them!

-4-
Life's more interesting when you listen

2019

I first heard the expression *"You have two ears and one mouth"* from a sales manager and proud Yorkshire man called Ian – so I'd always assumed it was something of a Yorkshire proverb. Later I discovered the saying probably had its origins not in Yorkshire but in another God's own County some 3,000 miles away; in a letter written by a man called James 2,000 years earlier; *"everyone should be quick to listen, slow to speak and slow to anger"* – now there's a challenge!

In the age of social media, the emphasis is on the posting (giving) rather than on the listening (receiving).
In this age of engagement listening is vital, without listening how can you possibly engage?

Customer Engagement, Customer Relationship Management, Voice of the Customer ergo Employee Engagement, Employee Relationship, Voice of the Employee... you get the gist.

When you actively listen as the Chinese character for listen translates, *"with your eyes, ears, mind, heart"* you'll learn far more than when you're talking.

Here are two instances, when remembering to listen helped me to save a customer worth hundreds of thousands of pounds and a marketing campaign thousands of pounds in material costs.

#1 Hearing the aside

Faced with fines from a major retailer for late deliveries and part orders, along with increased admin costs from the related invoice issues, we were in danger of losing business that had taken 3 years to secure. I got everyone involved with servicing the account round the table to walk the customer journey and we managed to identify a few small process issues, but it was the whispered aside *"but if there's not enough, I take them from x"* that revealed we had some KPIs that were working against each other.

#2 The silent listener

As a youngish Product Manager, I was working on a launch that was running late, and when my boss asked to see the target audience feedback on the point of sale, I had to buy time, divert budget, and hastily organise focus groups. The first of which I attended in the role of sample display builder, which I sat behind during the group session as a silent listener; out of sight and in silence listening to the group's views and opinions. Based on the *"I wouldn't stop and look at that stand but my husband would"* I changed the style and imagery, and I like to believe significantly changed the sales.

"When you talk, you are only repeating what you already know.
But if you listen, you may learn something new."
The Dalai Lama XIV

So, the Golden Rule for Leaders is to
"Listen twice as much as you expect others to listen to you".
The Value Innovator.

-5-
We only see what we want to see

2017

And we only hear what we want to hear because it suits us... it's easily done but aren't all mistakes!

Very often in looking for an answer we focus on everything that confirms that answer because it's easier, quicker, and less challenging but the answer you had in mind might not be the right answer for that particular situation.

Yet without the advantage of perspective and the willingness to watch and listen we can become quite myopic - the personal challenge is to hear everything and see everything.

In reality this becomes, see what you can, and hear what you can, question what you see, and question what you hear, including your own motives and decision drivers which are often framed by our own emotions.

Without this commitment your decisions can have quite a devastating impact on individuals, projects, and organisations.

Consider the following 3 scenarios:

Staff Appraisals
When seeking performance feedback from peers on a member of the team, the ill thought through comment driven by a lack of time, consideration and understanding or even personal agenda could shape

and form a perception that could take on a life of its own, especially if the originator of the comment was one of influence or position - as we know perception is fact. It could be a negative or a positive perception of an individual that could wrongly result in them being overlooked for promotion or over promoted.

Project Research
Which is at times is wrongly signed off to support the decision and dependant on how far down the timeline the "decision" is, determines the level of resistance to change.

As a young Product Manager I was working on a launch that was running late and when my boss asked to see the target audience feedback on the point of sale, I had to buy time, divert budget and hastily organise focus groups – I was guilty of seeing what I wanted to see / be seen (Hey Ho the arrogance/confidence of youth).The initial disappointment from what I heard, saw and read soon turned to gratitude as it led me to significantly change the imagery, which I like to believe significantly changed the sales.

Organisational Mergers and Acquisitions
Often fail to get across the line or go down to the eleventh hour for reasons that with hindsight appear so ridiculously insignificant. I was involved with one acquisition which didn't get across the line despite completing all the necessary due diligence and box ticking. Some years later I saw the Group FD who was involved at the time and asked him why it hadn't happened – amazingly it came down to him being "too busy".

No matter what role you have in your organisation you have a responsibility and an accountability to question what you see and question what you hear, including your own motives and decision drivers, without this commitment your decisions can have quite a devastating impact on individuals, projects, and organisations.

-6-
Engage your customers by engaging your staff

2015

Markets are becoming more and more competitive with new brands, products, services, initiatives, stores, and websites.

As a consequence, we all have to be smarter in our thinking and approach, as to how we want to be perceived by our customers, as ultimately, it's how we make them feel that will attract and retain their custom. It's true this is how the majority of us shop these days... according to how we feel.

We certainly remember the standout experiences - the good as well as the bad, but the vast majority of experiences are bland, and in today's social media world you can't afford to be anything other than BRILLIANT.

Put simply, you could have developed and invested thousands to have the best proposition in your market but if your employees don't believe in it or feel part of it, then your customers are never going to get it, understand it or importantly feel it.

Engagement is not just another phrase thought up by academics and consultants or something that just applies to the large multi-nationals. It is a term used to describe a business culture or approach that can and has made businesses of all shapes and sizes more efficient, more effective, and ultimately more profitable.

In 2014 a Financial Times survey of CEO's reported that

"Leaders of UK businesses stated that the two most critical challenges in delivering sustainable business success were employee and customer relationships and that employee engagement is a greater priority than customer service."

You know from your own experience that engaged individuals tend to:
- take fewer sick days.
- stay with you longer.
- work not only harder but smarter.
- are more committed to achieving their objectives.
- find more innovative solutions to problems.
- more likely to use their own initiative to do a good job, for you and your business.

Engagement ... you know it makes sense, but do you know how?

-7-
What's the purpose of a mind if you can't change it?

2021

Well, that depends on the context, doesn't it?

Take Politicians for example, we can all think of some who change their minds according to which way the popularist winds are blowing to save their seats and of some who hold so tightly to their opinions that they have fallen on their own swords – as we know perception is fact!

Yet in life there's a time for principle and a time for reason and the skill of a leader is in knowing the time and being prepared to face and make the choice.

Yet some don't want to change, some say they can't change, some aren't allowed to change, some don't know how to change, some have change forced upon them, some embrace change and some decide to change.

During the Pandemic it seems we've experienced all the above emotions in some context or other - lockdown, essential travel, remote working, no working, offered the vaccine, waiting for the vaccine, refusing the vaccine, following the data, then the date, then both; schools open, schools close, shops open, shops close (some for ever), missing the commute and now refusing to commute!

Effective change starts with the individual's decision to change, which is often the hardest part of change.

Muhammad Ali (the world's Greatest Heavyweight Boxer) once said.

> *"The man who views the world at 50 the same*
> *as he did at 20 has wasted 30 years of his life".*

You may not be 50 and you don't have to be 50 to feel you've wasted some of your life, particularly through lockdown. So, here's my question to you ... in the context of life's decisions around relationships, family, career, health, wealth, purpose, and wellbeing.

Can you list the number of times in the past 10 years, that you have significantly changed your mind?"

-8-
Good performers recognise the worlds changing and acquire new skills to ride the wave.

2015

In difficult times growth is hard to achieve and it is necessary to change not only the way you think but the way you behave - it's time to try something new.

How else will you find out what growth your business can actually deliver, without taking a different approach?

As Henry Ford is alleged to have once said, *"If you always do what you've always done, you will always get what you've always got."*

I often meet people who are looking to improve their business performance but refuse to change their approach or simply don't realise that they have to change their thinking.

How many businesses do you know are run by hamster wheel calendars, that risk producing cyclical trading years, the same old same old - its July again what did we do last July?

Such an internal focus limits a company's ability to notice market changes, consider alternatives and adapt. In some market sectors you *"can't just continue to do today's job using yesterday's methods and still hope to be in business tomorrow"* (Peter Schofield).

If you want to change the result, you need to change the way you do things.

15 years ago, I was a member of a board wrestling with the potential impact of the "world-wide-web" on our business. We could see the cost saving opportunities but were very concerned about the risk to our established business model and our customer reaction to any web-based service changes.

We decided to not only embrace the external changes but to be courageous and lead them in our sector, in order to secure the future of the business, rather than be responsible for its decline as the world moved on.

It involved tough decisions on many of the things that the business had been built on, and affected our people, products, and processes. Sites were closed; budgets moved away from traditional print to the new digital; knowledge and skill gaps had to be filled often via new recruits; and there were the inevitable redundancies. It was an unsettling time for everyone, especially as the only known apart from the cost, was what we could lose. It was a time when the traditional thinking of the old world met the new; and the hamster wheel experience in the business increasingly counted for less and less.

As a manager of a business no matter how big or small, you have a responsibility to learn, change, and adapt to secure the future of your business through continued growth and profitability.

You can read articles, papers, and blogs; you can attend seminars, workshops, and conferences BUT there comes a time when you have to walk the talk and make the change.

That's when you need to consider your position in terms of other priorities, physical resource, knowledge gaps, skill gaps and the potential need to utilise the experience and expertise of someone who can help you ride the wave.

-9-
Careers and Cocktails - now's the time!

2017

It makes more sense to plan your next move, when you are less frazzled, and away from the demands of the job. When you are relaxed and can enjoy the emotional and mental space that comes with a summer holiday (and cocktail).

Consider the 6C's of the Careers and Cocktails plan, that will help you start early and get ahead, whilst everyone else is snoozing in the sun.

1. Chill - do not feel guilty about taking time out of your holiday to reflect on how you got to where you are and where you want to be next year. (Holiday destinations included)

2. Context - the excess baggage you've brought with you, that's often-labelled stress, guilt, frustration, and disappointment – why did you pack them or rather who packed them for you and why did you carry them there?

3. Clarify - what you don't enjoy doing, what you enjoy doing AND what you are passionate about doing. Try and get to the very essence of what you want to do and write it down on one side of a cocktail napkin, then turn it over and think about...

4. Culture - consider the type of company culture you want to work in - the hours, the facilities, the decision-making process, the colleagues,

the flexibility, the adaptability, the responsibility, the engagement, the autonomy. Reflect on the cultures that have inspired you, either having previously worked in them, read about them, or been told about them. With what, do you feel an immediacy?

5. Company Sector - some avoid certain sectors, some target specific sectors, others believe they are only qualified to work in certain sectors. What about you? Often the happiest people are those who are working in a sector that they are passionate about ... as it never seems like work to them.

6. Catch Up - people are more relaxed and receptive to approaches in the summer, so start to think about the former colleagues, friends, and acquaintances you can reconnect with, who may be able to help you connect with those who are currently working in the companies or cultures you've just thought about.

Then fold the napkin away safely and order another cocktail – you've earnt it.

"Summertime when the living is easy...
One of these mornings you're gonna rise up singing
And you'll spread your wings and you'll take to the sky."

-10-
A career choice requires courage and confidence
2018

In the next 2 years 40% of people in the UK are planning a career change and are already working on their exit plan, and the 47% who do not find their work fulfilling owe it to themselves to consider an escape plan. (First Direct Bank 2018 UK poll of 2,000 people).

Whether it's an escape plan or an exit plan, both require courage and confidence to execute.

We all have choice but certain things like money, qualifications, skills, experience, mobility, contacts, courage, and confidence give us greater choice; whilst the lack of some of these things can make choices harder, it's often fear that is the most debilitating.

Yet you owe it to yourself, and your long-suffering family and friends who listen to your mumbles and grumbles, to at least define what you really enjoy doing, because if it's important enough to you then it's easier to make the choice.

Cliché Warning:
"Life's too short to be wasted doing something you don't enjoy".

Note to Employers - experience tells you that the exit planners tend to be the most able, who you should be looking to retain; and the escape planners tend to be the disengaged and the ones you should be giving wire cutters and shovels to.

The 3 biggest things that stop you leaving:

Golden Handcuffs.

25% of people in the poll said they couldn't afford to leave - so how much do you really need to earn, what are you prepared to sacrifice financially to secure your career change, future happiness, and career fulfilment. Or have you accepted that you are there just for the money?

You don't know where to go.

Then spend time on a self-audit to understand what you really want to do, the more you put in at this stage, the easier it will be to take decisions later. Importantly, decide whether this is a company change or a career change and start to plan accordingly.

Fear of the future.

After all the time and effort to get yourself into a position where you have an exercisable choice, you fear that the future may be worse than the present and you stay put. Logic will tell you, that you are not the only one that's been through this thought loop, and you won't be the last. So, find someone you have worked with and who you trust, that has already made a career exit/escape, as there are lessons to be heard from what they did and didn't do; as well as confidence and connections to be developed.

The next 3 biggest things that stop you leaving:

YOU don't have time to look for a job, then stay where you are as it can't be that bad; but one day your boss may hand you a pair of wire cutters and a shovel.

YOU think you'll never get through the interview process and hearing about some of the recruitment processes used by some HR departments I'd tend to agree. A friend's son has just gone through the following interview process for a £20k role: 1st stage online test. 2nd stage classroom test to check the online test. 3rd stage face to face interview. 4th stage one day group assessment. 5th stage face to face interview. 6th stage the offer. But if you're not in the process you'll never get to the offer stage.

There's much to be said for the Virgin Trains Onboard staff recruitment practice – *"here's my card if you're ever looking for a change call me; there's no need for a formal interview I've seen everything I need to see in your interaction just then with that difficult customer"*.

YOU don't have enough time or half day holidays left to attend the interview process… then it's not important enough to you and the escape plan can wait for another year.

We all have a choice YOU just need the courage and confidence to make it.

-11-
Managers and Directors should act like Owners
2022

My early work ethic came from weekend and holiday jobs working alongside family members in family-owned businesses (farming, serving chips, selling fashion) which clashed with the nationalised Christmas post round advice I received on my first morning before leaving the sorting office *"don't be back here before 11"*. The most startling advice I received was "No work, No eat" - not that surprising given I was volunteering on a commune in the south of France for the summer.

In hindsight, I believe I was recruited for my first "proper" job because of my (interviewed) attitude and behaviour - which were quickly formalised into how to take responsibility for my allocated area of business.

My direct line manager George Howard, 40 years my senior would often say things like
"a sale isn't a sale, until it's been paid for".
"Take decisions that are right for the business not you".
"Spend company money as if it was your money".

How should an Owner act?

1. Ensure they maintain a financially sustainable business.
2. Regularly remind themselves how many households rely on their employment.
3. Take responsibility for the actions / inactions of their people.

4. Never allow acceptable to become acceptable.
5. Learn from what worked well and what didn't work so well.
6. Ensure business processes and procedures are consistently applied and remain relevant.
7. Continue their own Professional Development - so they stay relevant.
8. Focus on adding value to their business through their people, product, and processes.
9. Encourage recognise and reward those who find better ways of doing things.
10. Allow people to fail - though not too often.
11. Remove the obstacles that stop people doing their job.
12. Create the environment for a culture that allows a business to "flourish."
13. Recognise their strengths and recruit to fill the gaps.
14. Get out of the way of the people they employed to do a job.
15. Inspire their people to think like Owners.

And finally, if in doubt ask those who have been there and done it - in my experience they are often extremely willing to help.

-12-

Are you a Holiday Wimp?

2015

According to a recent UBS survey the Japanese take fewer holidays (33% of their entitlement) and the French the most holidays (89% of their entitlement) with the Brits and the Yanks somewhere in between.

The survey stirred up memories of the 1987 film Wall Street and Gordon Gekko's *"lunch is for wimps"*, and I wonder if we are beginning to feel the same about taking our holidays?

In some organisations taking your full holiday entitlement could be seen as a sign of weakness or a lack of commitment to the job; in others taking less than your entitlement could be seen as a sign of insecurity or indeed inefficiency.

What's the holiday culture in your organisation?

In the last 3 years, have you?

Always taken your full holiday entitlement.
Interrupted your holiday to read your emails.
Called the office whilst on holiday.
Returned to work during a holiday.

Can you remember how each of the above made you feel?

Most of us fall into one of the following camps, those who profess to be too busy for holidays, those who look as if they always need a holiday, those who continually tell you they need a holiday and those who ensure they use their full holiday entitlement.

Which one are you?

I'd recently been at my desk for several hours and I decided that I needed a break (insert Holiday). I'd been working hard and deserved one… as I stood up to leave the following question interrupted my decision, *"how productive had those hours actually been?"*

AND here's the point…

I always take my full holiday entitlement and my best holidays have been those that have followed productive days, weeks, and months, which may have been long, hard and at times under difficult circumstances, but I was doing a job I liked, doing it well and felt good about it.

This meant when on holiday, I was able to immediately relax, sleep well, feel good, not be distracted, and dare I say good company. I remained confident and relaxed about what and who I'd left behind and what I'd return to, neither was I stressing over the final few days about returning to work.

Enjoy your Job … Enjoy your Holiday!

-13-
The Skills for Growth - were they developed or axed in your business during the recession?

2013

As the worst of the recession is reported to be behind us, focus is now turning to the lack of skills required for growth.

If it is to be believed computing, engineering, and manufacturing are all crying out for a skilled workforce to help drive the recovery, the need to convert our NEETS into Apprentices, and re-train our long term unemployed to be able to return to employment is topping the political, if not the boardroom agenda.

One group that doesn't seem to be attracting such attention are the senior managers, who after implementing rounds of cost saving initiatives also became a cost saving, as the recession forced businesses to re-strategise to survive.

In short skills, experience, knowledge, and expertise that served a business well in times of growth were lost at the top, as well as at the bottom of the pyramid.

So, the choice facing CEOs and MDs today is whether to train or recruit the necessary skills for growth, in order to exit the recession riding the wave rather than wallowing in the wake.

As an employer you would have supported your middle managers to fill the void by mentoring, training, and developing their skill set as future senior managers of your business, and whilst mindful of the old adage that it takes time to "put a wise head on young shoulders", you could now be well placed to exploit the opportunities of growth.

When updating your senior manager's skills matrix, you will have been cognisant of what skills will be paramount in driving your business growth in this changing landscape – and could still be faced with the same question of whether to train or recruit.

A question that needs to be answered, sooner rather than later, if you are going to ride that wave!

-14-
Your business may have grown, but have you?
2018

Rodney is 77 years old, and as we chatted it was clear he had experienced life - not in terms of the trappings of career progression and boardroom status but his grey hair, wrinkled face, and twinkling eyes said he knew a thing or two about life and the pearl of wisdom he hit me with…

> *"real growth is something that comes from the inside out Michael, it's not something you get at the gym."*

Which got me thinking about my own growth and the growth of those I had worked with over the years.

The experienced Sales Director with 20 years in the role that was little more than the same 2 years ten times over; or the wasted talent of the creative Product Assistant who with a little more application could have gone far; or the promising young Manager who failed to grow with the business. We've all met and known them at some time or other in our careers.

Growth isn't something you get from outside, but the outside can inspire personal growth.

You can attend every conference, complete every course, meet the great, the good and the inspiring but if you don't apply what you have seen and heard, you will be stunting your growth and wasting potential talent to become a *"better"* person, partner, peer or professional.

5 Self Growth Questions for you and your business.

Q1: How good is your community?
The people you chose to surround yourself with, what do you allow them to bring to you or the business... positivity, negativity, energy, fatigue, support, challenge, or the courage to say NO to you. Build a good community around you, listen, be receptive and act accordingly.

Q2: How much time do you spend interacting with those in their 20s?
There is much talk and coverage of engaging the younger generation of consumers.
It's probably more important to your business right now and your own development to learn how to engage the latest generation that are employed in your business.

Q3: When did you last apply something new in terms of your thinking and approach to the business?
Growth comes from your personal commitment to learn, adapt, and change as an individual. It is a journey just like the rest of life, so use milestones to check your progress and ensure you're not stuck on a roundabout.

Q4: Are you still trying to be the person you're not?
Authenticity is key ... to be true to yourself you have to know yourself - no I didn't get that from inside a fortune cookie, but the reality of understanding yourself will help you in the way you approach your people and your profession, and, in some cases, it may mean you make a company or career change.

Q5: What changes have you personally made in response to your biggest failure?
Learn from your experience, accept the responsibility of its wisdom and be the change you want to see.

-15-
Would YOU follow YOUR leadership style?
2016

Forget the words that spring to mind when you think of Trump, Mourinho or Corbyn, instead reflect on the emotions your style of leadership creates in those you lead. Do their emotions equate to how you describe your leadership style?

We all know about Leadership, read the book, done the course, and got the T-shirt; but how many of us are actually effective leaders in our organisations?

In my career I've worked for some inspiring leaders AND some not so inspiring bosses.

The optimist in me says no experience is a wasted experience - you can learn from everyone you work for, even if it's how NOT to do something! The realist in me has at times said, "this Boss is a hindrance to me, my colleagues and the business".

Our responsibility as business leaders is to inspire our people, not hinder them, to remove all the emotional and physical obstacles that stop them believing that the apparent impossible, is actually possible – not too dissimilar to parenting a child.

As parents (leaders) we want to see our children (employees) fulfil their potential in life (role) and we demonstrate some or all of the following cyclical actions when deemed appropriate for their personal development.

Such as:

> Encouragement
> Communication
> Direction
> Suggestion
> Demonstration
> Support
> Forgiveness

Today the concept of leadership is no longer dependent on position - being a director does not necessarily make you a Leader. The concept of leadership has shifted from command and control to inspiration and persuasion; people follow people, particularly those they respect and trust.

Jesper Nielsen (formerly of the global jewellery brand Pandora) speaking at the NAJ Congress on Inspiring Leadership said *"The leader in the room is the one with the most persuasive argument that gains the trust of those there"* – a business rather like a sports team needs lots of leaders on the field.

So how do you get this elusive respect and trust?

Well not the way I went about it in my first marketing managerial role - newly promoted from leading an external sales team and charged with adding greater urgency and customer centricity; I defaulted to command and control over a desk top PC ... yes, I know. I still cringe when I think about it, but I was young - even though the business case was sound, the delivery style set me back with my new team for quite some time.

To build trust, you must be trustworthy, this requires a habit of doing what you say you will do, and as I painfully learnt - doing it in the right way.

Be careful not to give undeserved praise just to make someone feel good or to use honesty as an excuse to express your anger - how often have you heard someone say *"I'm only being honest"* after delivering a severe blow to another's confidence and self-esteem.

Simon Sinek's Ted Talk "Why good Leaders make you feel safe" develops the theme of respect and trust.

In essence he says Leadership is about the creation of feelings NOT instructions *"you can't say to your people trust me and they will"* – they have to be persuaded by what they see you do and hear you say.

> *"When the leader puts people first and they feel safe and secure, and remarkable things happen".*

3 Questions and 1 Exercise to help you decide if your leadership style is one to follow:

Questions:

Q1. Do you adjust your style according to the person in front of you?

Q2. Do you encourage and support your people to take their own decisions and actions?

Q3. Do you remove their anxiety and fear and replace it with passion and direction?

Exercise:

For each question you answered yes, think of two examples that illustrate the frequency and significance of these leadership traits... for example you can claim to empower your staff but is that with the petty cash or the keys to the safe?

Post exercise question:

Would you still follow your leadership style?

-16-
Which voice dominates your business?

2022

I'm not talking about the customer voice, or the managing director voice but the type of voice, not whose voice, that tends to dominate in your business and the damage that can cause when other voices are not heard.

In these heightened days of increased employee engagement, collaboration, and cooperation in business generally or specifically in problem solving, sharing knowledge, or creating innovation, it's important that voices - all voices, are heard.

Where voices aren't heard or simply ignored; people feel misunderstood and undervalued, meetings become ineffective, the atmosphere changes for the worse, teams don't function as well as they could, the gossip starts, the sick days increase, and people eventually leave!

All of which diverts time, money, and resource away from you being able to lead the business in achieving its goals.

Once you recognise your own LEADERSHIP VOICE you can start to learn how to value the voices of others.

I was introduced to the 5 Voices of Power by Dale Parmenter of DRPG, a business Dale set up over 40 years ago and is today recognised as a leading full-service presentation and communication group, employing 380 people in 10 locations across the UK, Europe, and US. It's a business that has successfully embedded 5 voices within their culture, to help bring out the best from everyone. https://www.giant.tv/5voices/hq5v The premise of 5 voices is that *"everyone has a natural leadership voice, whether they know it or not, from the quietest to the most gregarious all have the ability to lead"*.

Our voice is made up of all 5 voices, some are just more natural to us than others, thus being aware of which of the voices are our primary and secondary voices can be extremely useful when speaking with others.

The 5 voices from quietest to loudest are:

Nurturer: 43% of the population who champion people, values.
Creative: 9% of the population - ideas, innovation, integrity.
Guardian: 30% of the population - due diligence, resources, processes.
Connector: 11% of the population - networks, communication.
Pioneer: 7% of the population - strategic vision, results, problem solving.

There are no right or wrong, better, or worse voices, this is simply a preference tool like Myers Briggs, which if used responsibly can help you improve and enhance your internal communication.

It'll be no surprise to those I've worked with to read that my primary voice is Pioneer, and my secondary voice is Nurturer - spooky stuff eh!

And now for some practical stuff, I recapped 5 voices with my peer2peer groups 7 months on from when they had first been exposed to it at a national conference, and the perception was one of *"it's something for the big companies with lots of employees, it's not for our smaller companies"* - which proved to be a tricky mindset to move, that's until 5 slides in, a voice at the table said, *"it works"*.

Alexis runs a business with 8 employees in the south of England, she was pleased that she was the only Pioneer *"there's only room for one pioneer in my business and that's me"*. The process also flagged up that she had too many Guardians one of whom was in the wrong role and a Creative demonstrating 'idealist perfectionist tendencies' when an 8 or 9 out of 10 was perfectly acceptable commercially. She now has a happier, more collaborative, and effective team AND at the other regional meetings I dialled her in at slide 5 - as businesspeople love hearing from other business people especially about what things have worked for them.

During a round table discussion, I was frustrated at being unable to move the meeting beyond a particular sticking point and encouraged an individual to *"work with me on this ..."* At the end of the discussion, I apologised to the individual before we all left the table for closing them down and for exhibiting a Pioneer trait - which led to a healthy discussion on using labels to excuse our behaviours... lesson learnt.

Peter runs a business with 15 employees in the north of England, he was initially disappointed that his primary voice was not a Pioneer, as often (and mistakenly) business leaders are expected to be Pioneers, aren't they?

Instead, he embraced his dominant Creative voice, understanding how it had helped him lead and develop his business over many years and then appointed an internal Pioneer to join the board, ensuring a potential imbalance was balanced.

Reflecting on my own experience (post 5 voices) I recognised that bringing out the best in others had been in the 'detail of my relationships' and not the broad-brush strokes of a leadership address to the employees.

-17-
Better Boss Better Business

2021

Being a better boss today is not just about delivering the numbers, it is also about how you deliver the numbers. How you adopt, adapt, and advance your culture and your purpose led strategy to incorporate everything from and to CSR, Diversity, Inclusion, Equality, Social Justice, Sustainability, Climate Change etc, along with the demands of Brexit and the Pandemic.

A Boss whether good or not so good, plays a huge part in how much we enjoy our work.

> *"Relationships with management are the top factor in employees' job satisfaction, which in turn is the second most important determinant of employees' overall well-being. Research shows that 75 percent of survey participants said that the most stressful aspect of their job was their immediate boss."* McKinsey 2021

Afterall, we have all heard it said, *"good people don't leave good jobs, they leave bad bosses"*.

Below are 4 easy to implement actions to help you become the change you want to see and a better boss in a better business.

1. Get rid of pointless policy and process.

The things that challenge common sense given our covid19 experiences - As a parent I learnt the value of asking myself in parent child situations does it really matter? If it does, address it. If it doesn't, let it go. Otherwise, risk jeopardising your relationships with employees, suppliers, and customers.

Imagine the easy to imagine situation when you receive a delivery that has duplicated the order quantities - supplier policy states the entire delivery must be returned and redelivered. Common sense suggests the required amounts are accepted signed for and the excess returned on the original delivery vehicle.

One that may be a little more challenging for the accountants, is the amount of time spent checking every expense item that costs more in time, than the items cost to purchase.

Remote working practices enforced on us by the covid lockdown, certainly torpedoed the long-held assertion passed down the generations of office managers that, *'one needs to be seen, to be seen to be working'*. It'll be interesting to see how the debate on remote or office working, within the context of mental health and wellbeing works out - one or the other, or a hybrid blend.

I once brought a colleague in from another office to review how we did things in head office. I announced it to the staff and made it clear that the purpose was to identify processes that added little or no value or could be improved through on the job collaboration. The project was called *Why do you do that?* Try it, you might be surprised at some of the answers and opportunities it raises.

2. Avoid the quick and easy option when it comes to succession planning.

Whether you are a family run SME, a large National or Berkshire Hathaway looking to appoint a successor to the 90-year-old Warren Buffet, head of his $650billion conglomerate; be very clear on what the role requires to not only survive but thrive in the future.

The emotions, practices and satisfaction of work have probably changed more in the last 18 months than they have in the last 18 plus years and the requirements looked for in a Boss needs to reflect that.
 It's less of the same old, same old, and more of the same, same, but different.

I can remember in my early days at P&G when I asked what I had to do to get promoted. *"Make yourself redundant Michael"* - an answer I only fully appreciated when being asked the same question by young guns. In short, once the business can function without you, then we can move you on, without risking the business you left behind.

I've witnessed directors make quick and easy appointments because it accelerated their career move, by sliding the wrong people into their soon to be vacated chair and in time come to regret it.

Similarly, siblings being promoted beyond their capabilities, without the infrastructure, support, or training to survive and thrive as parents decide to call it a day and head to the beach.

If *"bad leaders are the biggest risk companies face"* (Warren Buffet) then possibly *"good leaders who stay too long are not far behind"* (The Economist).

3. Be approachable, available, and an active listener.

Now this can be risky because it makes you responsible and accountable for what happens next. What you are going to do, with what you heard, and whatever your decision, you must respond.

I was once parachuted into an open plan commercial department from the Exec Floor – it wasn't officially called the Exec Floor but that's where all the directors offices were located, though I never discovered how the rest of the organisation referred to it - perhaps just the third floor (I hope).

My landing changed the dynamic of our previous team interactions, as now The Boss was looking over their shoulder or listening in on their conversations - or so it must have seemed, and no one performs consistently well if they think the Boss is watching them.

The silence was deafening! Gradually the banter returned, and with it the interruptions as staff felt they had to defer to me. There were jokey suggestions made about me wearing a hat or raising a desk flag when I was busy on something like a board report, customer strategy or next year's budget. Where previously meetings would have taken place out of sight in my old third floor office, we had a glass office constructed at the end of the office - known as the fish tank, it never quite worked as well but looked great.

Since then, studies of open-plan offices have shown that they do not create the hoped-for collaborative effects. One study found that face to face interactions fell by 70% in open plan offices, in the absence of a physical barrier people create a fourth wall - indicating their desire for solitude by facial expressions, headphones or curt replies to questions. (Bartleby)

The *'Why do you do that'* project, revealed an increase in email traffic between staff sitting at neighbouring desks, which had replaced previously held conversations following my arrival in the department. The project feedback also suggested that moving me off the floor into a corner office would be good for everyone ... and it was!

> *"Really good bosses listen and change the way they behave, perhaps enabling a much more independent way of working. You can't just tell people to work independently, you also have to change processes, such as how you're meeting, how you're communicating, to make that possible. For the boss, that can mean quite a bit of effort."* (Tera Allas)

4. Remove obstacles to performance.

Often translated to remove all excuses for a poor performance. In the budgeting process I often challenged my sales and marketing to people with *"in 12 months' time don't tell me you could have done x if only you'd had y - ask for it now and build it in."* Which went a long way to instil a sense of trust and confidence when it came to setting attainable objectives.

You may not have the budget that Pep Guardiola has at his disposal to produce the best football in Europe, but he is the first to recognise that everything possible must be done to enable the players to perform better than the competition in every game, in every way. From taking care of every off-pitch requirement (housing, gardening, transport, family, schooling) every aspect of training (physiotherapists, psychologists, dieticians, 1-2-1 coaching) to ensure every chance of a perfect on-the-job performance. (VAR willing).

A Better Boss makes every effort to make their employees' lives easier, physically, mentally, and emotionally, to enhance wellbeing, purpose, engagement and ultimately business performance. Better Boss Better Business!

-18-
Even those at the top need nourishment

2016

What's your diet like? Are you getting the necessary food for growth, health, and success? Are you building your immune system to cope with the pressure, uncertainty, and change?

If you are in a responsible position, you have a responsibility to yourself, your family, your business, and your employees - physically, emotionally, and professionally, and if you neglect yourself there is every chance that those around you will also suffer.

These feelings of responsibility tend to be more acute in smaller businesses where often the MD or CEO is the owner and main decision maker, and mistakes can be costly, even to the extent of threatening everything they've work for - mortgage, school fees, holidays, and the continuation of the family business. No one else in smaller businesses tends to feel that isolation in decision making.

> *"It is no longer about the lone male hero receiving applause for solving everyone's problems. Leaders need to allow those around them to shine, stop being fearful of saying 'I don't know' and allow different voices and opinions to be heard."*
> Dr Tobias, Cranfield University

Yet Bosses don't like to share such apparent weaknesses and vulnerabilities particularly to those who may exploit them. Anxiety and sleepless nights over an issue or required decision can take on gargantuan proportions of uncontrollable aspects. How often have you gone home worrying about a member of your team that did something wrong, when it's them that should be worrying about you?

> *"Loneliness does not come from having no people around, but from being unable to communicate the things that seem important to oneself, or from holding certain views which others find inadmissible."*
> Carl Jung

Who is going to tell you that you are no longer making something better, just different?

Business Mentors are not just the domain of start-ups and the under thirties – they are more than a Red Adair (external problem solver) or personal coach, they can be a confidant and in time a friend who supports and challenges, listens and debates, guides and facilitates.

Thomas Chapman's dissertation on CEOs in the health service concludes that
> *"CEOs perceive high value in being with other CEOs for one-on-one, informal group interaction, and for having access to a congregation of CEOs in a unique group setting."* - In modern parlance Networking.

Being too busy is no excuse for not changing your diet - we all manage to find time (sometimes selfishly) for the things we regard as being important AND your performance should be just as important as the business performance. Otherwise, you may become another victim of the Peter Principle.

The principle that members of a hierarchy are promoted until they reach the level at which they are no longer competent, everything they know and regard as tried and trusted no longer works in the more challenging situations. They have reached their "level of incompetence" and seen their last promotion.

Nourish your personal and professional development - don't become another Peter!

Dietary Advice that will improve your health, growth, and success:

1. Control your diary - don't let it control you.

2. Invest in improving your own performance - not just the performance of the business.

3. Don't assume 20 years' experience is the answer - it may be one years' experience twenty times over.

4. Network - find people who you feel are similar and commit the time and effort to building trusting supportive relationships.

5. Create work free zones - manage your holidays and weekends.

6. Consider a mentor - it's good to talk.

-19-
It's time to reset your Leadership compass

May 2021

During the storm that was covid19, good Leaders quickly and decisively altered their course and their style to lead their businesses and teams through the unknowns and uncertainties of the pandemic.
Many excelled in supporting their people physically, financially, emotionally, mentally; as well as championing changes in their businesses to ensure the business would survive the storm in some shape or other.

The vaccine and the Prime Minister's roadmap now signal the time for a business leader to reset their leadership compass, as we leave behind the fear of yesterday and look to the hope of tomorrow.
Whether employees have worked as normally as possible through covid, or remotely or been on furlough, when they return with their colleagues to their place of work, they will be looking less for empathy and more for direction – **employees will want to understand the roadmap for the business and what it means for them.**

Before a roadmap can be shared, considered, and adopted, it needs to be written; and a good place to start is with the answer to the question, which changes will endure?

Consider the changes the business may have witnessed, experienced, or implemented in terms of sector, suppliers, customers, costs, people, product, and process.

For example, will all employees want to return from remote working, do they need to return to their pre-covid place of work? In terms of the hours of work, can they also be flexible? Can certain roles continue to be fulfilled (and fulfilling) outside the normal place of work in the normal hours of work?

What dormant skill sets, and behaviours will need re-energising - sales conversations, time keeping, in person (off screen) meetings?

A good road map allows a Leader to clearly set out for the employees, the direction of the business, the goals, plans and activities, and importantly clarify the expectations the business has of each employee, in terms of standards, behaviours and attitudes – in short what it means for them.

-20-
Do YOUR people know what GOOD looks like?

2017

You may have told them but depending on the how and the when you told them, they still may not know what your expectations of them or the business are.

As we know from life itself - GOOD to one person may mean something entirely different to another person's GOOD; and that's how issue starts, in the failure to agree what GOOD looks like at the very outset, so we'll all recognise it when we get there.

The issue becomes even more subjective / emotive / difficult when the definition of GOOD is applied to individual qualitative performance rather than the straightforward hit this number and we will have had a GOOD year!

Imagine the difficulties when writing standards of performance or signing off job descriptions or setting objectives or worse still, appraising someone against any of the above if you have an undefined GOOD.

Make life easier for yourself (and your people) by providing examples of what GOOD looks like for each competency, objective, or procedure; and yes, by default what every other rating looks like too, from unacceptable to excellent.

Here's what one of my appraisal definitions looked like in my first job back in the 1980's … and I'm sure the wordsmiths out there will have refined one or two things since.

Problem Solving & Priority Setting

"Identifying problems & opportunities, drawing accurate facts & figures to make presentations & quotes, quick & accurate in usage".

Interestingly, today's thinking when it comes to performance rating is to have a five-point scale, as ratings affect the employees' perception of fairness. A study by Bartol et al, reports a five-point scale resulted in employees being more confident that they could improve their performance, set higher goals for themselves, and went on to see higher rating improvements. Whilst a three-point scale may be deemed too hard to be worth the effort for a move up from a 2 to a 3.

My employer in the 80's only had a three-point rating scale:

Significant Strength,
Strength,
Needs Improvement – in other words if it wasn't a strength you needed to improve!

BUT perhaps the most important takeaway from these 400 words on what GOOD looks like is to ask your people and agree with them what GOOD definition should be applied to their roles, objectives, and the business they work in.

-21-
If experience doesn't meet expectation, YOU lose

2015

I'm concerned that I've morphed into Victor Meldrew (a grumpy old man) *"I don't believe it!"* Over the last 2 months my normally happy experience in some of my local businesses was not so happy - my experience did not match my expectation. Expectations that had been formed over previous 'contacts' and I believe it was down to people not keeping their brand promises. Emotion still drives our buying habits, and we like to feel good, when we hand over our money.

This mild Victor Meldrew rant is about recognising that if you have the wrong people in the wrong jobs, you will damage your business - believe it!

Here are some of the not so good, bad, and rather ugly experiences I had recently that all involved young people who I believe have either not been trained or have forgotten their training; have not received any ongoing support or received insufficient support; or were recruited for the wrong job or put in the wrong job. As the old adage says, "we are only as good as our people" and that applies to people of all ages.

Award Winning Restaurant - after a couple of mouthfuls of the wonderfully presented starter I looked like a 2-year-old who had applied their mother's lipstick and quickly tried to wipe it off with the back of their hand before being discovered, much to the initial amusement, then concern of our group.

"Excuse me, are there any nuts in this starter?"
"Why do you ask?"
"er look at me" exit stage left to the kitchen returning 3 minutes later to say
"I've spoken to the Chef, and he says the oil he used was very hot and it was probably just too hot for you".

I don't believe it! So, what can we learn from this?

Make sure your people are encouraged to ask questions of others in your organisation and not just accept the first answer they get if it sounds ridiculous or they don't understand it.
Ensure your customers get all the relevant purchase information they require and do not treat them like clowns even if they look like one. I have since learnt that they use nut oil which is now flagged on the menu.

International German Car Brand – outside the showroom at 7.25am I and two other brand owners were waiting to drop off our keys and disappear whilst our cars were serviced. Moments later the service team walked on to the showroom floor indicating the start of the day, one of whom took the long slow walk towards us, attempting no eye contact or verbal acknowledgement. Even when they arrived at the door, they just activated it, turned on their heels and walked back to the service desk with the 3 of us following 5 steps behind in silence. Once seated behind their desk they said, "Hello Mr Donaldson how nice to see you again".

I don't believe it! So, what can we learn from this?

Treat your customers like people not appointments or machines that get switched on when you are ready to start. A simple "Good morning come on in" at the door would have been sufficient to engage us, especially at that time in the morning.

Multiple Retail Optician - I have shopped at this store for over 20 years and really value their service and expertise, so this experience hurt. Long multi-visit story cut short, I broke the arm off my glasses and had to hold them together with a relatively discreet tape, as I took them in to be repaired whilst I waited - surely it wasn't a big deal.

They returned from the onsite lab with one-inch-wide brown parcel tape on the arm which came away from the lens when I put them back on. The *"You cannot be serious"* quip was lost on the young staff member who had probably never even heard of John McEnroe.
My *"you really expected parcel tape to hold a delicate arm to a lens"* was met with *"our technicians do not carry out repairs, if you want them repaired it will take 7 to 10 days and cost £130, what do you want us to do?"*.

I don't believe it!

I left to shop the other opticians in the town, only to return a few days later wearing some very old glasses found at the bottom of a draw and handed over my money and broken glasses. A week later I returned to collect my repaired glasses and was presented with them inside a branded pouch. After a few days of wearing them, they didn't seem quite right, on closer inspection the newly fitted arm was shorter than the original arm.

I don't believe it! So, what can we learn from this?

Well aside from the obvious be more careful with your glasses. Always treat your customers with respect even if they may be a little agitated and always confirm that the customer is happy with their purchase before they leave.

Independent Shoe Shop - I wanted a particular style of shoe that they didn't carry in stock but could order for me from their supplier, unfortunately they arrived marked - to which the young person's response was "it will wipe off with a little polish when you get home".

"I'm sure it will but just to be sure will you do it for me now", they tried and failed, much to their embarrassment. Then I got the natural leather blemish line - what they didn't know, is that I had worn this brand of shoe before and had been searching for this particular style for some time, so probably knew more about them than they did. But they did know that I'd wanted to break them in before a particular occasion, so I was not best amused when they said they could send them back and get another pair but there was no guarantee they would be any different, now I'm being squeezed. Then they offered me a discount equivalent to 0.78% of the purchase price

I don't believe it! So, what can we learn from this?

Train your people to interact with your customers, to engage with them, to make them feel good about their purchase and NOT to automatically default to the sales manual, apparently, we can get intuitive robots for that.

And finally ... if you are going to take six minutes to make two cappuccinos whilst talking to colleague at least remember to add the coffee!

So, what can we learn from all of this?

If experience doesn't meet expectation, YOU will lose customers and their custom. Recruit your young people on attitude and behaviour, then equip them with the knowledge and skills required to provide the experience your customers expect because as we all know - the experience is in the detail.

-22-
The Male Pale Stale Board
2019

Now that's what I call an entrance, though it may not have endeared her to 90% of those round the table and it may have been instantly dismissed by the majority as unnecessary and perhaps even provocative, but it made me think - at the expense of missing the following exchanges, (aka banter) as I mentally marked myself against being:

1. Male - tick
2. Pale - she has a point I've not seen the sun for months.
3. Stale - ouch

I know it could have been her nerves or perhaps her icebreaker on entering a room full of males (in 2018 there were just 30 women in full-time executive roles at FTSE 250 firms, down from 38 in 2017) but at that moment in time, I was ruminating about the stale.

I don't regard myself as stale, and like the other male, pale and stale/s in the room I had invested in that day's Leadership workshop to avoid becoming stale!

What does your board look like?

Prior to life as The Value Innovator, I worked for some very large companies in terms of turnover, employees, sites, countries, and sat in boardrooms for 20 years AND in all that time the average board was 81% male and pale but not necessarily stale.
But I would say that wouldn't I - Turkeys voting for Christmas or those in power voting to change the electoral system – it's not going to happen!

So, here's my back of the envelope **7 question Stale Test** for you to (more) objectively assess the health of your boardroom - Turkeys and Politicians need not participate!

Q1. Length of time each individual has spent on the board.

Q2. Relevance of their expertise to the needs / future of the business.

Q3. Breadth of their experience - could be a single years' experience repeated over and over for the last 7 years.

Q4. Demonstrable willingness to learn, improve, develop, and embrace change.

Q5. Contribution to the business outside their functional responsibility.

Q6. Effectiveness as a board member - company & sector knowledge, communication skills, wisdom, and vision.

Q7. Take full Cabinet responsibility for the difficult decisions as well as the popular.

There may be lots of reasons why your board has become male, pale, and stale; but that need not be the case - the most effective boards are those that evolve to meet the needs of their stakeholders, employees, and customers.

-23-
I'm the Monster my Boss created
2017

Six words uttered by my boss that concluded a disappointing conversation on a proposal that had been rejected by their boss. I've only ever heard them once and we never referred to them again and yet they have remained with me for years.

Six words that said all that was to say about the culture of the business, the creator (the big boss) and the created (my boss)... the sense of helplessness, the lack of control, the inability to influence, feelings of being trapped in the role by the money, the fear of leaving, or even the desire to see it out to the end, despite the obstacles and the inability to let it go.

There are countless surveys supporting the claim that *"people don't leave jobs, they leave bosses"* but what about those they leave behind, those who fall into the "happy to stay" and the "unhappy to stay", and those too fearful to exercise something we all have … CHOICE.

Here are six challenges for the Frankensteins and the Monsters in your organisation.

Six challenges for the Creators - the monster makers.
1. Recognise how much you set the "mood" within the business.
2. Work on creating a culture that makes people want to stay.
3. Live the values that will motivate and inspire people.
4. Manage performance regularly and positively.
5. Look for strengths over weaknesses.
6. Build genuine relationships.

Six challenges for the Created - the monsters
1. Recognise that these values are not yours.
2. Remain true to who you are.
3. Avoid taking the misery of work home.
4. Do not allow the culture to become your excuse.
5. Recognise that your boss may not want to change – they may be a perfect cultural fit.
6. Exercise something we all have ... choice ... and answer The Clash, Classic Conundrum *"Should I stay, or should I go?"*

-24-
Essential advice from non-essential business owners
2021

In a world that has been turned upside down by the pandemic we need leadership and purpose.

What is one person's non-essential is another person's essential. In this context, try explaining to a small business owner that their business (and for many their livelihood & life purpose) is non-essential. When only essential journeys are allowed, why are non-essential businesses allowed to offer click and collect for non-essential items. Such is the fog and frustration.

Through the months and months of lockdown and tier enforced closures, owners of non-essential businesses have shared with me, their experiences of being closed, of having too much time on their hands, of zero sales of home schooling and 24/7 relationships.

Here's the advice gleaned from those conversations, that potentially ALL business owners need to hear or be reminded of, not just those deemed non-essential.

Spend time on your business - never again will you get so much time away from the day to day of the business to work ON your business, so make it productive.

Understand your business numbers - walk through the what ifs and the potential impacts on your business, post grants, post furlough and reduced customers.

Understand your positioning in the sector & locality - who are you and what do you bring?

Focusing on the threats, could cost you missed opportunities - get your head up and plan for tomorrow.

Identify the habits & behaviours that have got in the way - work on the those you are going to change, either by doing them less or just stop doing them.

Spend time with your trusted network - the one thing we all have more of (at the moment) is time, so invest some in the relationships you value.

Embrace digital - it will improve your business resilience.

Engage your community - support your physical and digital community where you live, work and play; encourage them, share their posts, and buy from them.

Love yourself and love what you do - the loss of purpose, relationship, routine, income, and wellbeing have affected people's self-esteem and confidence. Remind yourself of life before lockdown and plan the positive change you want to be.

Remember to make money - it pays the bills, pays the wages of others, and gives you business and life choices.

In a world that has been turned upside down we need leadership and purpose.

-25-
How putting people first improves profits

2016

Anyone can cut costs to improve their profit but once it's cut its cut; it requires greater expertise, courage, and a particular culture to be able to deliver sustainable profit improvement.

Cliché Warning
"you are only as good as your people".

The essence of a good business is having good people; support your people and they will support you or as the multi award winning media company Mediacom proudly promotes on their door plate.

"People first, better results".

80 years ago, The John Lewis Partnership got it right when they wrote their purpose statement:

"The partnership's ultimate purpose is the happiness of all its members – through their worthwhile and satisfying employment in a successful business".

Today this business employs over 90,000 people between the ages of 18 and 83; and has (profitable) annual sales of £11Billion.

Put simply, you could have developed and invested thousands to have the best proposition in town but if your people don't believe in it or feel part of it, then your customers are never going to get it, understand it, feel it or importantly buy it.

Cliché Warning:
"the profits in the people detail".

I recently spent a weekend in a 4 star London hotel owned by 'the global leader in hospitality', hospitality which extended to informing me via an acetate guest notice blue tacked to the inside of the lift about my weekend breakfast – you know late, lazy and relaxed over coffee and the papers: *"we suggest you enjoy our breakfast before 8.45hrs as our restaurant gets extremely busy between 8.45hrs and 11.00hrs"*, and it only got better.

Briefly and I mean briefly...

I asked for the shower screen to be cleaned on arrival - this was not done. At the breakfast podium I was informed breakfast was not included and was sent to reception to sort it out myself by the 'podium police'. I brought the receptionist back with me to prove it wasn't a system error but a stressed staff error along with the suggestion that they provided their staff with more training and support. (No, I wasn't pitching).

In the afternoon I phoned the spa and ended up speaking to someone at reception, (as they no longer staff the spa area), who didn't know if lockers and towels were provided, and failed to tell me to take a pound coin with me. Once there and changed I found the steam room was out of service and the sauna was OFF, in my shorts and flip flops I set off to find the duty manager, who offered to have the sauna switched on.

In the evening I was running late, the invite said 7.00 somehow, I had got it in my mind it was 7.30 and it was now 7.10 so I phoned the concierge and asked him to secure a taxi and hold it on the meter... I would be 5 minutes I was there in 3 minutes to watch him open the taxi door for someone he had mistaken for me - it took 10 minutes to get another taxi.

The following morning, I was woken by housekeeping at 10.15, check out was midday!!

The highlight of the stay was being pulled out of the privileged members queue by Veronica, who speeded my exit but not before I answered her question "have you enjoyed your stay?" ... I even rejected a complimentary night because I don't want to stay there again!

Clearly in this particular business the decision to protect the profits by cutting people costs has resulted in some being extremely disappointed with their customer experience, that they can't even give rooms away free of charge!

What a different story it could have been had the management grasped the culture of people first better results, instead they have fewer people, busier covering tasks previously performed by those no longer working there and have lost sight of their very purpose - hospitality.

Result - people costs down, customer satisfaction down, brand value down, future profits down... if only they had put their people first.

-26-
How many game changers do you employ?

2016

If 78% of game changers - those who effect significant shifts in the current way of doing or thinking about something, have left companies to work for themselves, what type of employees remain?

The survey by eg.1 on the DNA of Game-changing Teams goes on to quote Steve Jobs and his Think Different speech in 1997.

"Here's to the crazy ones.
The misfits.
The rebels.
The troublemakers.
The round pegs in the square holes.
The ones who see things differently.
They're not fond of rules.
And they have no respect for the status quo.
You can quote them, disagree with them, glorify, or vilify them.
About the only thing you can't do is ignore them.
Because they change things.
They push the human race forward.
While some may see them as the crazy ones, we see genius.

Because the people who are crazy enough to think they can change the world, are the ones who do".

AND most times they are a pain to manage because they don't readily conform to the traditional business structures, hierarchy, policies, and procedures; they keep jumping out of the box!

As a result, they tend to be labelled as risk-takers, perfectionists, visionaries, mavericks, disruptors, villains, dysfunctional, non-conformists or simply too much trouble; and are often sacrificed for an easier life or for a safe pair of hands that will continue to do what we've always done.

BUT with a sponsor they can make a real difference as they see things before others, they have imagination and vision; they are not deterred by failure and strive to solve problems.

They thrive in a culture where it is safe to fail and are praised for trying rather than criticised for failing.

YET the key to organisational success is getting all these individuals working with others, as one collective team, and that's what good people managers do!

To survive and succeed Game Changers need a sponsor in the business - are you sponsoring a game changer in your business?

-27-
Are you too busy doing STUFF?
2016

I once shared a board room with Gimli, the dwarf warrior from Lord of the Rings and his gruff, in your face *"its stuff, just stuff"* mantra. Initially the other members of the board assumed it was a quirk of character but gradually it began to irritate and grate, as he frequently challenged ideas and suggestions with the outburst of *"its stuff, just stuff"*. Unfortunately, just like Gimli his delivery style tended to stop others hearing the message that: your stuff is a distraction and indulgence that stops you focusing on the things that make a real difference in the business.

How often are you just too busy doing stuff IN the business, that it stops you doing more important stuff ON the business?

20 years not long after AOL had made email widely accessible as a communications tool, I looked up from desk to see my MD standing in my office - he wanted to know what was so important on my screen that I hadn't seen him enter. *"I'm clearing my emails"* to which he replied something along the lines of, *"you won't be needing your secretary then, remember I don't pay you to type, I pay you to hit your budget!"* and walked out - message received loud and clear!

How often do you find yourself just doing stuff that is expected, inherited, or requested of you, irrespective of its value contribution?

We are all guilty at times of doing stuff that we shouldn't be doing, the nice to do stuff rather than the need to do stuff. Some wear the 'I'm busy badge' with pride, I'm indispensable, I'm important, yet a full diary and a full in-tray says more about one's efficiency and effectiveness.

Northcote Parkinson's laws around the issues of efficiency and effectiveness remind me of two stories that illustrate how easy it is to be too busy doing stuff.

Law#1 "The man whose life is devoted to paperwork stuff has lost the initiative. He is dealing with things that are brought to his notice, having ceased to notice anything for himself".

I recently made a social visit to a client I had completed some work for six months earlier and over a coffee they begin to share with me how well things were going, how the team had adopted the changes and the positive impact it was having on their numbers. At which point I noticed two key totals didn't correspond - long story short - they had been too busy doing the report stuff that they hadn't cross referenced it with a related report.

Law #2 "Work stuff expands so as to fill the time available for its completion".

After decades in stock control, it came time for Gary to retire and leave behind his daily task of compiling a materials report. Several weeks later the FD found himself in the stock control office (no he wasn't lost) and noticed Gary's vacated desk was piled high with candy stripe printouts - long story short - because no one had been using Gary's report for any real value when Gary left no one noticed that Gary's report was still being produced, not even the guy from IT who every morning added today's candy stripe data on top of yesterday's candy stripe data ... and we had gathered everyone together to say good bye and give him his 'gold watch' - I hope Gary never got to hear about his life's work.

Solutions to Stuff…

During my time at Williams Holdings, a successful FTSE 100 company that acquired and turned round underperforming businesses; I was told to only have one 'thing' on my desk at any one time, that being the 'thing' I was working on. Which when practised did limit the distraction of stuff, though on the occasions of surprise visits my desktop was rapidly emptied into my desk draws!

There is nothing wrong with doing stuff as long as it's the right stuff, the trick is identifying the stuff that no longer adds value and letting go of it.

You could start by only having one thing at a time on your desk or employ a Lean Six Sigma expert to help you or employ a team that doesn't create stuff or translate the lessons from production efficiencies to the offices or for an immediate low cost, high value impact ask some simple questions of yourself and your colleagues.

1. Is this stuff still required?

2. Is this stuff still relevant?

3. Is this stuff still adding value?

If your answer is anything other than a resounding YES, review it, revise it, or just stop it and start doing the stuff that adds real value to your business.

-28-
The Ideal Employee and the C word

2019

Not all Boards function efficiently, effectively, and professionally. Surprised? No? Good! AND it usually comes down to the people, followed closely by the lack of appropriate process.

In difficult trading times the cracks of underperformance are harder to paper over, passengers easier to spot and tensions more obvious - the usual response is a reactive one of board away days, which are not always guaranteed to deliver the desired outputs and not always guaranteed to run smoothly.

On one such away day we'd covered company charters, employee statements, customer statements, vision, and values - all bundled up by the C word CULTURE.

Open discussion had led us to considering the type of people we enjoyed working with, and the type of people we would like to work with in a high-performance team. Very quickly we had a white board full of the attributes, behaviours, and cultures of The Ideal Employee - the ABC's.

> *"Why do you look at the speck of sawdust in your brother's eye and pay no attention to the plank in your own eye?"*
> Matthew 7 v3

Now it was much closer to home, more than an exercise, more demanding and more revealing.
By the end of the day, we had a list for the Ideal Director in a high-performance team and more importantly we had agreed to take our senior managers through the same process and compare our respective lists.

At the end of the company wide process, we had involved our people in rationalising 3 very long ideal lists for employees, managers, and directors down to ten ABC's on each; and agreed a common 4 ratings key (performance score) the bottom one being "development opportunity".

We had ensured that everyone felt that they had had the opportunity to contribute and recognised, that although the culture had been instigated from the top, the wider organisation should be able to feed into it thus creating a two-way street, ownership of a common goal and in turn a shared culture, for working in a high-performance company.

Unsurprisingly, many of the ABC's were duplicated across the lists and just tweaked to reflect the role, for example: Team Player and / or Leadership. The lists were available to all employees and actively used to support, encourage, and challenge behaviours within the business; and formed the basis of the company's appraisal system, which in turn generated some real conversations that benefited all 3 parties - you, them, and the company.

To help keep the ABCs in the minds of my team - especially at the times they might have been tempted to complain and blame others around them. I bought them each a small pocket size compact mirror which sat on desks and in top drawers with the pens, post-its, mints, ibuprofen, and staplers and said everything that was required in two words **Ideal Employee?**

-29-
This is the self-preservation society
2015

How big is your company society?
There may just be one or two individuals or there may be enough to form an unofficial self-preservation society, with members from all levels of the company, including the management. Where they exist in numbers, they can have a quiet but stifling effect on the business and before you realise it, the business rather like the coach loaded with gold bullion is teetering over the edge of the cliff, rocking backwards and forwards but never quite enough to go over and never quite enough to regain any forward traction.

How do you spot members of the self-preservation society?
Well, it can be difficult if you've been with the company for some time, as you've probably developed a blind spot to their ways. It is much easier for someone new or from outside who has more recent experience of how other companies' function. But here are a few tell tail signs to help you scope the size of your company's self-preservation society:
Members make their work fill their day.
Not a minute more not a minute less, yet they are always busy.
Heads down, Hands down two things' members never do is lift them up.
Silently resistant rather than constructively commenting.
Years and years of experience, but the same few years ten times over.
Silos are their natural habitat; they offer them protection and longevity.
More often defined by their title, than by what they actually do.
They warm seats, drive desks and are happily engrossed in emails.
New starters don't stay very long - well the ambitious ones at least.

In my experience there are 3 options: Leave. Live with it. Change it. Which one will you choose?

-30-
Don't go breaking my heart
2022

It's February and love is in the air, well so say the Valentine associated businesses of confectionery, flowers, restaurants, cards, engagement rings etc. Which got me thinking about the people who tell me how much they love their jobs - be that in person, a biography, an interview, article, or LinkedIn post.

I'm not talking about taking pride in their work or caring about what they do or their purpose but about being passionate for what they do, where they do and who they do it with.

For an SME business owner, passion is a vital ingredient for success, but applied in the wrong quantities, in the wrong mix, at the wrong time, it can break not only the heart but the results.

In fact, passion should carry a wealth warning.

If you don't have passion for the business who is going to drive it forward, and if you have too much passion, there's not only a risk to the business but to yourself and those around you.

For those in creative sectors it's hard not to be passionate about being passionate, and it's certainly more appealing than dealing with the mundane demands of the business such as cash flow and the P&L.

Effective leadership requires self-awareness particularly when it comes to engaging both brain and heart.

Self-awareness helps you avoid recruiting in your own likeness, it helps you secure complementary skills not duplicated skills and it appreciates the value add of employee diversity and inclusion. It also helps you remember to reward performance not perceived passion.

Passion is not just the domain of brands and marketing. Passion stops you playing it safe, it pushes boundaries and increases expectations, engagement, and exposure.

Passion gets you through the start-up and scale upscale stages of your business, as well as bad days at the office.

But passion should carry a wealth warning because it can:

- Stop you getting your head out of what you are doing.
- Cloud your judgment.
- Limit your decision making.
- Get you too involved with personalities and dramas.
- Give priority to the process rather than the result.
- Overwhelmed those around you.
- Increase the levels of emotion in a business.
- Stop you going home on time.
- Interrupt your family events, weekends, and holidays.
- Distract you from what pays the bills.
- Stop you delegating.
- Stop you stopping.
- Stop you starting.
- Stop you growing.

Passion can be self-indulgent, but Passion CAN improve the P&L, especially when channelled to achieving the opportunities of greatest business value.

-31-
Happy or Content - Asked the President

2021

At the time I was paying more attention to the grilled plaice just placed in front of me to have heard the start of the conversation, but I then clearly heard the voice of my client's President *"Let's ask the Value Innovator what he thinks."*

My food musings had distracted me from a conversation being held 5 or 6 seats away about the difference between staff being content and staff being happy, and now all eyes were fixed on me.

Both are emotions I offered, and one is very steady and the other comes in waves (grilled plaice is best eaten hot). *"Ah perhaps you'll share more in your next Value Innovator blog if you do requests"* (now I stopped taking requests when I stopped DJ'ing at Uni but why let an explanation get in the way of a hot plaice).

Let's eat!

As we passed in the hotel reception the following morning on my way from breakfast, I was pleased to inform the President I'd accepted his request and had already nailed the first fifty words and chosen the image - of a grilled plaice of course.

These are certainly emotional times, and our pandemic associated emotions seem to be playing havoc with so many lives, business plans, relationships and teams, and business is about people is it not; and people are emotional beings.

We don't want robots, but nor do we want a workplace dominated by emotions, they can be distracting, destabilising, and damaging both professionally and personally.

Every team needs a balanced mix of emotion, with dominant emotions coming to the fore in required situations, for a business to thrive. For example, new product development is better served with passion than contentment, based on the Cambridge English Dictionary definitions below:

Content - pleased with your situation, and not hoping for change.
Happy - feeling, showing, or causing pleasure or satisfaction.
Passion - something that you are strongly interested in and enjoy.

As a business leader you'd be happy leading your employees from contentment to passion - wouldn't you?

This transition starts as it does in every good company at the top.

Cliché Warning:
*"You and your leadership team need to become
the change you want to see",*

That means creating the right culture and environment for your people to become passionate about the company they work for - they need meaningful not meaningless work, a shared sense of purpose and a role they enjoy day in day out.

I know from my career I've been happiest when working with likeminded, passionate, people.

-32-
Has the internet killed the sales professional?
2018

I suppose I first learnt the art of sales from Bob-a-Job week, from there I started my own car washing business which was me with bucket and sponge in hand, knocking on neighbour's doors and offering to wash their cars - in time I developed a price list based on size of car and size of house. I progressed from picking strawberries in a field, to selling strawberries from a farm stall, then on to working at the coolest clothes shop in South Manchester... Jack Price owned and run by Mr Jack Price. An elderly gentleman with two sons, two shops, one market stall and a lifetime in selling - he taught me about people's habits and behaviours; that years later would be formalised when I joined Procter and Gamble - known at the time as the university of marketing.

35 years on and I'm still refreshing my sales practices by attending seminars/days hosted by sales professionals like Phil Hesketh, Gavin Ingham, Lee Lawson and Steve Edge.

Why?

Because I'm aware that the world is changing and increasingly becoming a world of cyber interactions, screens, clicks, videos, soundbites, and elevator pitches.

What used to be done face to face is now done in cyber space, especially when people are looking for low cost and convenience. The demographic of the audience (and buyers) may have changed, the rules may have changed but the sales basics of meeting needs has not! Particularly for products and services that cannot be easily supplied over the internet.

And yet so many business owners and managers, ignore the sales basics when recruiting salespeople or moving internal people into sales positions. Opting for the quick fix, the easiest option, the cheapest option, industry knowledge, company experience etcetera etcetera.

At one workshop I discovered that many of those attending were one, attending on the instruction of their Boss and two, had recently moved into sales from other disciplines: a retired accountant that had been recruited as a business sales development manager, a creative agency director was now out on the road as a sales account manager, one after 23 years in the national health service was now an advertising sales executive, and an architect who recognised that he was a designer not salesman, was now a salesman.

Pause for Thought... desperate times require desperate measures... NOT SO they require measured measures, especially when recruiting sales generators to future proof your business in these changing times.

Here are some of the professional sales basics to look out for when making your next appointment:

Sales is a profession not a career optional extra.
Sales professionals are brilliant listeners not just persuasive talkers.
Sales professionals make it easy for people to say yes.
Sales professionals are engaging problem solvers.
Sales professionals are resilient and make people feel good.

-33-
Project success depends on your Process Jockey?

2016

Every project requires a jockey - someone who rides the process to the end, over hurdles, round the bends, through the field, across the finishing line and hopefully into the winner's enclosure.

I first heard the term 'Process Jockey' in a casual conversation with a friend who heads a team of project managers in financial services; I'd never heard it before but immediately got it.

Various dictionary definitions of Jockey include:
- a person who pilots, operates, or guides the movement of something.
- to struggle by every available means to gain or achieve something.
- a person "Jockeys" something to control or manoeuvre an item or challenge.

I digress, but I'm sure you get the concept of Process Jockeys.

So many project managers are process jockeys; they follow every step and every stage of the written process across the finish line but still don't get into the winner's enclosure.

For some unknown reason the project did not deliver the expected outcome, the goal, the objective, the very purpose of the project - it's not about getting to the end of the process (round the course).

Projects are not an end in themselves; they are a means to an end.

Back to my friend who has witnessed on a number of occasions qualified project managers struggling to explain at the project "wrap up" why the project failed and at the same time falling back on the bemused phrase *"but we followed every step of the process"*.

What factors contribute to a failed project?

Processes give you the best-known steps for success, but success is not always guaranteed as the process may be out dated and no longer fit for purpose.

The project brief may be lacking in detail, clarity, and deliverability and not fit for purpose.

Things change in the life of the project especially the longer the time frame, and factors often beyond your control can come into play and the process and the brief are no longer fit for purpose.

OR you might just have the wrong Jockey.

Why are Process Jockeys so important?

A Process Jockey with the experience to recognise change, the confidence to suggest change, the competence to effect change, and like champion Jockey Pat Eddery who had more than 70 rides before riding the first of his 4,633 UK winners, the character to get back on the horse and go again, is more likely to get you into the winner's enclosure.

Experience is Key

Often there are not enough projects on the go within an organisation for a Project Manager to get this type of experience.

One very good reason why someone looking to build a career in Project Management may need to move to difference companies and sectors to ride different horses on different courses, and why companies may have to recruit external Project Managers to get into the winner's enclosure.

-34-
Are your Marketers' T shaped or I shaped?
2017

With opt-in GDPR on the horizon data bases are going to be decimated, marketing plans torn up, and marketers reshaped.

Have you got the right shapes for success in your marketing team?

I first heard the T-shape term at a digital conference in 2013 during a presentation by a marketing recruiter who used it to illustrate their difficulty in finding the type of candidates their clients were looking for - marketers who had a broader marketing experience (T shape) than the digital only/specialist/biased marketers (I shape).

At the same conference I shared round table discussions with enthusiastic digitally qualified marketers bemoaning the fact that their managers didn't get it, trust them, or respect them and consequently would not support their proposals when it came to allocate the marketing budget.

Fast forward towards 2018 and my client experience since, suggests that this disconnect still exists in many organisations, particularly those challenged with reductions in their marketing budgets. This could be down in part, to a generation gap, the transition from off line to online activity but probably has more to do with tangible financial results, i.e., delivering the budget!

In the world of open rates and click through rates we could conveniently forget or fail to relate them to the ultimate purpose of every commercial organisation - to increase profitable sales. After all, this is what pays the staff salaries and shareholder dividends.

Here are ten steps to help you avoid being seduced or intimidated by the technology, blinded, or manipulated by the data, and to position you to maximise the digital opportunity:

1. Recognise that digital metrics are a means to an end not an end in themselves.

2. Be very clear on how digital fits within the overall strategic marketing plan.

3. Set clear means-to-an-end objectives.

4. Involve your I shape marketers in the broader marketing plan.

5. Commit to developing I shape marketers into T shape marketers.

6. Question the data you don't see - it may tell you more.

7. Get your I shapes off their screens and in front of customers.

8. Don't leave your customers behind.

9. Don't get left behind by your customers.

10. Embrace the lessons of failure and move on FAST.

How to improve the profitability of your PRODUCT

This is the shortest P section in the book due to client confidentiality, but I hope there is enough content to trigger your own product reviews.

-35-
How SUSTAINABLE is your USP?
2016

Commonly understood as a unique selling point or proposition, widely accepted as a defining point of difference, and often misunderstood on two critical aspects - unique and sustainable.

Most businesses are unable to claim a UNIQUE selling proposition and fewer still a SUSTAINABLE one.

Unfortunately for suppliers (not so consumers) in today's commoditised world where new products and services can and are copied in weeks, it's increasingly difficult for companies to identify a genuine USP, let alone sustain it.

What is your Unique Selling Proposition?
The term first appeared in Rosser Reeves book 'Reality in Advertising' over 50 years ago and was explained in 3 steps.

1. Every advert must explain what specific benefit you get from the product.
2. The product or brand proposition must be unique in the market.
3. The proposition must be good enough to attract new customers.

Many have forgotten or chosen to ignore the meaning of the word "unique" and settle for the oft used words of service, quality, delivery, stock, price, and choice. Today these are all taken for granted by customers and consumers alike, as they no longer differentiate you - even honesty and trust no longer count, after all which company do you know of admits to being dishonest or untrustworthy?

However, in the absence of a USP to be able to excel in the areas of service, quality, delivery, etc can set you apart from some of your direct competitors… but for how long?

How sustainable is your Unique Selling Proposition?

Assuming you have identified your USP, that it's understood, owned internally, and persuasively communicated externally; how long will you be able to claim that it's unique to your company before it becomes just another commoditised me-too?

Todays' search for real USPs is proving as difficult for consumers to find, as it is for companies to identify; and as a result, consumers especially the Gen Zs, are seeking out companies with which they can feel an affinity, based on authenticity, transparency, engagement, and responsibility.

Yet many companies will be overlooked as they have failed to identify, understand, and communicate their SUSTAINABLE UNIQUE selling proposition – a management process that doesn't have to be complicated.

-36-
What makes your business so special?

2014

Your business is not special if you simply deliver what you say you will deliver.

What is it that you do that keeps your customers or clients coming back to you rather than going to your competitors?

What are your real differentiators?

Often businesses I work with are shocked and disappointed to learn that what they stand for, that is their values, do not really differentiate them from their competitors.

Today, values such as service, quality, range, price, and choice are all taken for granted, even honesty no longer counts as such, after all which business do you know of, that admits to being dishonest.

If you dare to get beneath your initial list of things that you think makes your business so special, how many are genuine differentiators and how many are simply "me-too"? You too could be shocked and disappointed.

Your differentiators could be your people, products, processes, premises, location, brand or even your business philosophy (aka culture). In a commoditised world where products and services can and are copied in weeks, it's increasingly important to be able to differentiate yourself if you are going to attract, retain and grow your customers and ultimately your business.

-37-

Carpet

Pre 2013

A carpet business was several months behind its budgeted launch date for a new carpet that had significant numbers attached to its success. In fact, it was even in danger of missing its peak sales season in the months leading up to Christmas.

The industry tradition and practice was to present the product, order bespoke sample sizes and hope they would be put on display either by the staff of the store when they were posted out 6 -12 weeks later or by the company salesman on his next visit.

The challenge here was to ensure the product was on sale in store before the peak sales period.

Michael immediately actioned production of a free, pop-up display stand accompanied by the requisite samples, marketing materials and point of sale in advance of a launch conference.

Internal and external sales teams were motivated and incentivised to make this the first launch of its kind in the industry and to hit the original targets set. The external team arrived in their cars and left the sales conference in transit vans loaded with 50 kits each; the first displays were positioned within three hours and the first order received within an incredible twelve hours of the conference finishing.

In all, over 500 displays were positioned within the first week. The buzz within the trade was unprecedented with the internal sales team rushed off its feet opening new accounts and taking orders for displays from customers who had not yet seen their local salesman and, most importantly of all, the product sold over £1million of carpet in its first six months.

-38-
Great Products or Great Marketing - which one matters the most?
2014

When great products suffer from poor marketing, they never become best sellers!
    "Wow that's fantastic, why hasn't everyone got one?"

Can you imagine the emotions of the management when they heard the buyer say that about their product! I for one didn't know whether to cheer or cry as I heard it - delight for the recognition given to the product, and frustration for the lack of awareness.

The *"why hasn't everyone got one"* for me, was a double-edged sword... It's so good everyone should have one -v- what's wrong with it, if after all this time everyone hasn't got one? On reflection the buyer had raised as much doubt in that exclamation, as they had enthusiasm.

The finger was well and truly pointed at the marketing team...
Why hadn't this buyer seen or heard about this product in the last 4 years it had been on the market?

Apple is almost as famous for its launch marketing as it is for its product innovation. Pandora's marketing transformed a common bead into a global jewellery brand. P&G's marketing teams transformed a failing Oil of Olay into a $2B+ Olay brand.

You can have a great product but without marketing it will never sell - The two have to go, hand in hand with equal importance, if you want a best seller.

-39-
Remember everyone is an expert in Marketing
2014

Wise words from an MD over 20 years ago as we drove away from our Divisional office having just pitched a TV campaign to the Divisional board.

Earlier in the day I'd learnt the importance of 'knowing when to bite your tongue' when the Divisional MD announced the advert needed a jingle at the end of it, *"you know like that little red phone that drives over the hill sounding its horn in a catchy way... de de de de deeee."* (Direct Line Insurance) and there you had it!

He couldn't explain why the ad needed it but, in his opinion, it was lacking something and that was a catchy finish of some sort.

Before I could respond I'd been kicked under the table by my MD sitting alongside me.

This was at a time when the majority perceived marketing to be about selling stuff with colourful packaging and catchy TV advertising, at a time when everyone was exposed to hundreds maybe thousands of marketing messages every day, which qualified them as experts. Today, it would be the same as someone qualifying as a Social Media expert on the strength of a Facebook account and LinkedIn profile.

Marketing as the youngest of the traditional seats around the boardroom table, for which you needed no formal qualification to practice and is continually morphing - yesterday products and services, today engagement and experience, and as it's so hard for many to define, this in turn only creates doubt around its actual value.

Marketing has suffered from a smoke and mirrors image, in part by over selling the dream known affectionately as 'spin' but also through the overuse of 'jargon' which has made it more difficult for some to understand - it's too conceptual, compared to Finance, Production or Sales.

"The only known in marketing is the cost" along with the oft repeated quote from Lord Leverhulme, about *"half the money I spend on advertising is wasted"* has made the marketing budget harder to defend and it's still seen in many organisations as a discretionary budget and the first to be cut in recessionary times.

I much prefer the quote from Henry Ford who said,

> *"a man who stops advertising to save money,*
> *is like a man who stops the clock to save time".*

Marketeers, if you remember everyone is an expert in marketing, then your life will be less stressful, and far easier if you practice the 5 principles of KYC.

Know your Colleagues.

1. Listen
2. Acknowledge
3. Respond (in plain English)
4. Keep it short
5. Offer to follow up outside the meeting, when you can share a little more of the science of marketing with less of the subjectivity!

-40-
Customer Shoes - Walk in them to better your business.
2018

Have YOU ever bought a product or service from your own company anonymously, and experienced the highs and lows YOU give your customers?

Having walked a customer journey in your own company could you hand on heart recommend your company (based on your experience) to a friend without fear of it embarrassingly affecting your friendship?

To walk in your customer shoes, only takes an open mind and a little time, assuming your processes are efficient and effective; you can use a different name, you can even send it back, so it doesn't have to cost you anything, yet the experience could save you money and make you money by making your business a better business.

Sometimes it's enough just to share the experience to generate those Ah Ha moments when all becomes clear in terms of what you should be doing or not doing... charging too little for an exceptional service or charging too much for an appalling quality... where you need to remove the glitches or celebrate the joy.

Better People Experience means Better Business.

Late last year I travelled though Bristol airport for the first time, and what a pleasure it was - inexpensive parking within 200 metres of the terminal, through the automatic scanning barriers to the automated baggage drop, then on to security where we had our first touchpoint with airport staff, who were simply keeping the flow, flowing and into the lounge for breakfast. End to end it was the smoothest departure transit I've ever experienced and yet I found myself decrying the fact people were being replaced by machines!

Then we came to board our orange plane and it was sheer chaos ... so much for express channels and orderly boarding, it was a scrum, with people from all directions descending on the departure gate, boarding the plane from both ends, bringing the aisle traffic to a standstill, and then forcing oversized carry-on bags into the overhead lockers, only for the stewards to insist they are place in the hold. In all it took over half an hour to simply get 100 or so people seated – far longer than the time it took from leaving our car to getting our breakfast.

I then found myself decrying how people can get in the way of effective and efficient processes by not following them!

A simple *"Good Morning Everyone we are going to board by rows 20 to 30 from the rear steps, all over sized bags will be taken from you on the tarmac and put in the hold"* – it's not rocket science, but apparently beyond the wit of the men and women dressed in orange.

Better Process Experience means Better Business

Earlier this year I ordered several doors from the leading online building supplier - the lack of product specification (how complicated can doors be) prompted a call to their service desk which, 3 calls later resulted in them providing me with the phone numbers of two of their suppliers, so I could get the information I required from them myself!

In total this one stop shop resulted in three separate deliveries, from two separate suppliers, one incomplete quantity and two deliveries that required home access and a signature... Oh and I had to inspect everything within 24 hours, or the goods could not be returned?

Now whilst this company Board may be happy with the online stats and bottom-line performance of their business; just imagine the benefits of having walked in this customer's shoes – their corrective actions would not only boost their stats but their OP.

Better Product Experience means Better Business

Recently a family member had a bump in their car which resulted in it being collected by the red car insurance company for £3,000 of repairs at one of their approved repair contractors. In the meantime, the policy provided a replacement car through one of their approved car contractors – for the one week the damaged car would be away.

And so, the three-week saga began, for unbeknown to the red car insurance company their approved contractors were sub-contracting the work out to secondary unapproved suppliers.

A pick-up driver drove over a neighbour's garden, the car provider reclaimed the replacement car within 3 days because they had sold it and wanted it back, then left a second replacement car that was unfit for purpose. The repaired car was returned with additional damage and incorrectly fitted parts which meant it had to be returned for further repairs. It was finally returned two weeks later than promised with an additional 119 miles on the clock and in the dark – so it could not be inspected (so it wasn't signed for). At one point we had two replacement cars parked outside for two days, and our diaries had to be changed to accommodate a total of SIX car delivery and pick up dates.

Now before you say - you get what you pay for, or you should have gone to a more reputable company, this product was provided by THE leading UK car insurer perhaps one that has become too big and too busy collecting premiums to regularly review the product their brand has been providing and is certainly in need of walking in their customer shoes - more often than I suspect they do.

-41-
Conditioner

Pre 2013

An innovative new fabric conditioner was at risk of being delisted by major UK grocers shortly after its TV launch.

The cause?

Poor sales, high warehouse stocks and increasingly negative feedback from stores to Head Office.

The reason for the poor sales was quickly identified: the packaging was comparatively small and lightweight which meant that, when located alongside large displays of detergent it was lost, damaged or too small to communicate reasons to buy.

As a result, local store managers were demanding credit notes for damaged product, relocating it away from associated product displays to obscure areas of the store and demanding the removal of excess stock.

To address these issues, though no trained designer, Michael designed a display dispenser rather like a chocolate machine, to accommodate large quantities of product, protect the packaging, provide adequate scope for messaging, and sit snugly within the displays.

The product survived.

More than that, it thrived, and it's still available instore to this day. (Global Sales of $284m in 2013)

-42-
Demand For Greater Marketing ROI

2021

According to McKinsey research, (June 2021) 78 percent of CEOs are now banking on marketing leaders to drive growth, as more and more company results suggest that those companies who continued to invest in marketing throughout the pandemic performed better than those who didn't.

> *"Fulfilling an ambitious growth mandate requires a marketing agenda that is far more sophisticated, predictive, and customized than ever before"*
> McKinsey

As we went into lockdown a lot of companies responded as many respond to market downturns – they cut what they (mistakenly) perceive as discretionary spend; they cut their marketing campaigns, cut their marketing staff, replaced experienced (expensive) marketers with (cheaper) junior marketers; and now they are wondering where their growth is going to come from.

To compound the catch-up, there seems to be a shortage of qualified marketers: *"Marketing job vacancies more than triple since height of pandemic"*. Recruiters are reporting a trend for those *"who can do everything, from strategy through to delivery"* with a focus on *"ready-made candidates with experience"*. There's no time for training and development, businesses need a return on their investment and fast!

> *"We are seeing heightened demand for marketing directors as businesses continue to transform, including launching into new markets, driving growth, and pivoting around their customer propositions."* Marketing Week Oct 2021.

Even the companies that performed well during the pandemic are losing their star performers to excessively inflated salaries, as the scramble for the best talent accelerates. Yet they not only face challenge in terms of staff shortages, rising salaries, rising campaign costs, and increased competition but from new players, new brands and new play books!

Leaders of all businesses whether large or small will be looking for less risk and greater certainties on their marketing spend and with the acceleration of e-commerce during lockdown, there's so much data available, that today's marketers can no longer wing it with Lord Leverhulme century old quote. *"Half the money I spend on advertising is wasted; the trouble is I don't know which half"*.

I shared a boardroom for many years with a finance director whose pet phrase use to be *"the only guarantee with the marketing plan is the cost"*. They now embrace (digital) marketing. Why? Because it gives them less risk and greater certainty.

With all the available data a bad month can become a better month with a little carefully directed and timely spend, when a sales director's forecast sales shortfall can be recovered by a marketing director's digital spend - as the data enables them to forecast with greater accuracy than ever before the additional sales for every marketing pound spent - the FD loves it, who wouldn't!

As an SME you may not have a team of marketers, you may not have a transactional website, you certainly don't have a lot of data and your marketing budget was cut. But you are no different to the 78% of CEO's who want to drive growth and maximise the return on your investment, but are you looking to marketing to drive that growth for you?

The marketing principles of the BIG companies (if not the budgets) can be applied by SMEs, if their Leaders have a mind too, and it doesn't have to be that technical or complicated - there's lots of (free) helpful, shared data, experience, and information out in cyber-space. For example, Google Analytics 4 is making it *"easier to discover actionable, privacy-safe insights from across the customer journey, that you can use to improve your marketing from acquisition to retention".*

Marketing strategy, like all other strategies does not have to be complicated just developed and deliverable!

Here's a story I heard first-hand from the owner of a small family business who at the time had no e-commerce presence and a limited marketing budget which they regarded then as they do now, as a vital spend not a discretionary spend, but they weren't sure how effective it was. So, they contacted their customers with a simple 4-question survey, the fourth question was *"How often do you expect to make a significant purchase (value specified) from us?"* The answer to that question told them they could not turn their marketing activity on and off, and that they had to have a consistent and enticing presence in the sector. The answer to the other 3 questions told them with which channels to best engage their customers. They now have an annual A4 one sided Marketing Calendar with activity by channel, by customer segment, by spend and by expected return.

> *"While broad reach, powerful, resonant storytelling, and creativity remain critical, marketers now need to utilize data and analytics to enable more targeted and engaging interactions to shape consumer behavior."* McKinsey

Continue working on your story telling, creativity and channel content but recognise there's an even greater expectancy on the effectiveness (ROI) your marketing activity generates - which you ignore at your own peril.

-43-
Performance or Market improvement - where's your GROWTH coming from?

2020

The markets are under attack - *"Covid-19 presents the greatest danger to the world economy since the financial crisis of 2008"* (OEGD).

"The FTSE 100 fell more than 8% in early trading as fears of a global recession grew, caused by the impact of coronavirus and an oil price war - it is more than 20% below its recent peak seen in January when it traded above 7,600 points. The drop follows a 30% slump in the oil price overnight after Saudi Arabia launches a price war, as it boosted production amid a major disagreement with Russia. It is the biggest single drop in the price of oil since the first Gulf War, in 1991." (The Business Desk)

Closer to home businesses, both large and small are beginning to be affected by these macro threats.

The John Lewis Partnership saw profits plummet by 23% to £123m for the year ended 25 January 2020. *"We need to reverse our profit decline and return to growth so that we can invest more in our customers and in our partners...this will require a transformation in how we operate as a partnership and could take three to five years to show results."*

(Sharon White, partner, and chairman)

This morning, I received notification that an event I was due to speak at had been cancelled due to the threat of the coronavirus. Where's your growth coming from this year performance, or market growth?

I doubt it'll be the latter unless you have a magic lamp or an incredible plan like no other for said volatile markets, the still to be negotiated Brexit trade deal, the running saga of the US election and the daily status updates on Covid-19.

Studies by Management Consultants McKinsey support the assertion that business performance improvements can help companies survive market downturns. *"It turns out that in times of crisis and in times of economic slowdown, not everybody fares the same. When we traced the paths of more than 1,000 publicly traded companies, we found that during the last downturn, about 10 percent of those companies fared materially better than the rest. In short, your business context is and will remain uncertain. But if you get moving now, you can ride the waves of uncertainty instead of being overpowered by them... (this) requires big moves: dynamic resource reallocation, disciplined M&A, and dramatic productivity improvement."*

In Value Innovator terminology, focus on the improvements you can affect in your business today - improve the performance of your people, the profitability of your products and the productivity of your processes.

Realise their latent value, build their resilience, and transform your performance in these difficult times – it is far easier to control your controllables than the uncontrollable externals; and it doesn't have to be complicated!

#1 Improve the performance of your people.

Work on your communication skills – when people feel stressed by things beyond their control, they need to hear from you. They need to hear (and understand) what actions, initiatives and support you are intending for the business. In short, they need you to lead.

Training doesn't have to stop but it may have to change to reflect the changing needs of the market – whether that's online, in print or in person.

As well as encouraging employees to acquire new skills (both hard and soft) it's important that they are rewarded for these efforts. These soft non-technical skills are much harder to replicate via automation and AI.

Address the "problem children" that you've been too busy to do anything with or about.

And ensure your customers remain at the heart of your strategy.

#2 Improve the profitability of your PRODUCT.

Review your supply chain - as early as January UK manufacturers were feeling the pain caused by suspended shipments from China. If you haven't got a supplier strategy create one; you can start by identifying any over reliance on any one supplier/country and identify secondary suppliers for the same product but from a different country – *eggs in one basket* and all that.

Pass on your price increases – retain your customers via your improved communication skills.

Improve your new product developments or existing product enhancements – be driven by speed to market and adding low cost, high value improvements.

Exit the loss makers – it's a simple rule, if you can't reduce the cost and can't increase the price, then it's time to let it go.

#3 Improve the productivity of your process.

Review how you have you responded to increasing internet sales in your sector – are you getting your share?

Walk each, and every process, whether that's in administration, in the call centre or on the shop floor. Identify opportunities to remove bottle necks, reduce costs and increase efficiencies.

Journey map your customer touch points with your business, look for opportunities to reduce their pain and improve their experience.

Understand and share your data to make meaningful changes to the business in the areas where it will have the greatest impact.

Review your Social Media metrics beyond likes and clicks to ones that relate to revenue.

Score your existing communications process against these key questions.

> How open are you?
> Do you have an open-door policy?
> How aware are you of yourself?
> Do you remember to listen?
> How regular are your staff meetings?
> Do you seek feedback and suggestions?
> When did you last act on the feedback / suggestion?

Done well, these actions will encourage a positive culture change throughout the business in which everyone understands how their actions can add sales, cash, value, and growth to the business they work in.

-44-
Jewellery
Pre 2013

A chain manufacturer produced a lightweight pendant chain for manufacturers & wholesalers and a heavyweight chain for retailers to sell as purchased.

The lightweight product was seen as a commodity and a secondary purchase to the pendant. The heavyweight product was suffering from declining demand due to a shift in taste, compounded by a tarnished "Del Boy" image.

The challenge facing Michael was to increase sales and grow margins by becoming the chain of choice.

The target markets were the mass jewellery producers in the Far East and the independent jewellery retailers in the UK.

A key issue was changing the perception of the manufacturer in the two target markets.

A support programme based on stock availability, colour consistency, performance, product innovation, retailer approval and open book costing led to chain being sold to the key jewellery centres of Mumbai, Bangkok and Hong Kong and resold with a pendant in the UK and US markets.

In the UK, the heavyweight chain was repositioned within a new comprehensive range of jewellery that carried the chain name. Alongside the retained best sellers, new chain styles and weights were hung with pendants. Collections were sourced on a make or buy decision, exclusive partnerships were established with global brands

Disney and United Colors of Benetton, along with European brands Alice and Bruce. Up and coming UK designers were featured and their collections stocked and sold.

Additional staff with jewellery sales experience were recruited to provide retailers with a professional, knowledgeable, and inspiring range presentation.

Within 2 years not only had the sales volumes improved but so had the margins.

-45-
Ditch print at your own risk!
2015

In the digital scramble not to be left behind, many companies are forgetting the basics of marketing when shifting catalogues from print to digital. The simple truth about printed catalogues is that they are relatively expensive, but they work because certain customers like them.

I know it can be difficult to swim against the tide of opinion and the pressure on marketers from competitors, peers, agencies, boards and even their own cv, to follow the digital trend can cause channel myopia.

A decade ago, I came under intense pressure to cut costs (aka the print catalogue) and by demonstrating to the board the customers purchasing process - the cuts were found elsewhere. We were able to show that the sales of our company products were generated by the paper catalogue found in our customers' workshops and not by the computer found in our customers' offices.

That experience reminded me of 3 marketing basics:

1. Understand how your customers use your catalogues.
2. Digital is only one of many potential customer interactions.
3. Customers will choose how they interact with your business.

If you haven't seen the brilliant IKEA catalogue advert (ensure you google) *"experience the power of a book - at only 8mm thin, and weighing in at less than 400g, the 2015 IKEA Catalogue comes pre-installed with thousands of home furnishing ideas."*

In the UK major catalogue business like Littlewoods, Argos and N Brown are constantly reviewing their strategies against the landscape of lower digital costs, shareholder value, management changes, product sectors and customer demographics. In the digital game of pontoon, it's a case of twist, stick and fold.

Littlewoods have been sending catalogues to homes for over 80 years, at one point hitting 25 million, yet they have recently decided to drop the famous Littlewoods Catalogue in favour of a monthly magazine format.

N Brown CEO Angela Spindler has said that there are no plans to scrap its catalogues. *"I don't want to get rid of catalogues completely. It's a great catalyst and a great marketing tool."*

Argos has been driving a digital revolution in their traditional catalogue stores replacing print catalogues with iPads – however some stores are said to be restoring the laminated paper copies as customers prefer to flick through.

Digital has taught Print some key marketing lessons, with the latter embracing improved storytelling, infographics and strong visuals, all of which seen to be working, as there has been something of a catalogue revival in the US (Ulbe Jellume - Print Power Europe) and apparently the 25 year olds in Australia prefer to read catalogues in print than off line; where over 70% of consumers keep catalogues in their homes for over one month and 34% for up to a year. (ACA)

Whichever way you choose to interpret the data there is only one way to sense-check your decision and that's with your customers.

-46-
Trade Fairs ... All Marketing and NO Sales

2013

Exhibiting at Trade Fairs can cost tens of thousands of pounds if you include stand design, build, space, services, marketing, product, travel, accommodation, subsistence etc and I know it prompts debate in the boardroom when the final orders are counted.

Last week I walked several miles up and down the aisles of two leading international trade fairs, the Autumn Fair International and International Jewellery London, combined they boasted over 2,000 exhibitors launching over 60,000 new products – a quite considerable investment in NPD alone!

From my conversations with exhibitors, the days of covering your costs with orders are long gone but, in many companies, this remains the single most important criteria used to judge if the fair was a success.

Trade fairs are no longer just about writing orders on the stand, they provide companies with the opportunity to reach their target market with a variety of value-added activities that should be incorporated in their attendance objectives, such as:

1. Securing buyer feedback on potential activity.
2. Informing and building trust.
3. Competitor benchmarking.
4. New customer acquisition.

5. On trend focus.
6. New product launches.
7. Showcasing how best to present your brand in store.
8. Networking and connecting.
9. Market research.
10. Confirming follow up appointments.

Plus, the opportunity to assess if your pre-fair marketing activity worked or not, which on one occasion worked too well and prompted the organisers of a fair to close our stand by 1pm on the first day due to aisle congestion, health and safety concerns and competitor complaints. Fortunately, we were relocated to a larger space in an adjoining hall, in time for opening on the following day. It did however mean one member of our team had to remain on the vacated stand to provide directions to our new location – we live and learn!

-47-
Strategy doesn't have to be complicated - lessons from car makers

2019

May 2019 Press Headline: JLR (Jaguar Land Rover) British luxury car brand to be purchased by French PSA Group (Peugeot Citroen Vauxhall) just shows how quickly their respective fortunes have changed.

In 2014 JLR posted profits of £2.5B and PSA was rescued from BANKRUPTCY by new boss Carlos Tavares - within a year PSA was back in the black.

In 2018 JLR revenues were £26B with £1.5B profits and PSA revenues £64B with £2.8B profits.

'Peugeot Citroën DS has made significant progress for the 5th year in a row and is closing the first phase of the Push to Pass strategic plan with outstanding results. This demonstrates the ability of our Group to deliver a profitable and recurring growth. We are now entering in the second phase of the Push to Pass plan with confidence in a context of even stronger headwinds. No doubt that our agile, customer focused, and socially responsible approach will make the difference.'

Carlos Tavares, Chairman of Groupe PSA Managing Board Feb 2019

The essence of the PSA Push to Pass strategy is one that could be applied to almost any business:

1. Focus on profit not sales or market share.

2. Cut the products that make little money or no money.
3. Reduce production costs by culling product variants.
4. Acquisition agility when considering new Technology.
5. Invest in collaboration rather than capex for new geographical markets.
6. Engage the workforce with purpose and profit.
7. Never forget the customer - do it for them.

Business strategy doesn't have to be complicated, but it does involve you in some tough decisions about the future shape of your business and in particular, answering the key questions of what business you want to be in, how you're going to achieve your goals and what impact it will have on your people, product and process.

> *"Mindful of the key changes called for by the car of the future, Groupe PSA's strategy for 2016 to 2021 aims to make the Group a global car manufacturer on the cutting edge of efficiency and a provider of mobility services favoured by its customers.*
> *Driven by the Push to Pass profitable organic growth plan, this strategy is underpinned by three levers: The digital transformation of the Group. The internal performance culture. Corporate social responsibility."*
> Source: PSA Groupe

But the REAL VALUE comes from the implementation of the plan, and that's another skill set!

-48-
Appliances

Pre 2013

Michael joined a struggling business in the knowledge it was struggling, just how much it was struggling became apparent by the end of his first month.

6 years of reported operating losses totalling £47m, the loss of 45 sales and marketing staff in 5 years, a £6.5m loss on £42m sales in his preceding year, but then he was always up for a challenge in the belief he could make a positive difference.

In his first year he focused on the product, selling 244,000 units of obsolete stock through a managed channel for £4m and discontinued 200 products, which accounted for 60% of the remaining range. Low margin sales were reduced from 32% to 3% of total sales. Loss making terms of trade were renegotiated and operating losses were reduced by 80% to (£1.3m).

In his second year he focused on the product, 50% of the range was replaced with higher priced, higher margin product which was supported with 98% on time, in full delivery.

Then he focused on the people - 66% of the sales team were replaced with more professional account managers, product category management was pioneered in the industry via the sales, marketing, and logistics teams.

Then he focused on the process - Partnership strategies were established with key Distributors, resulting in a 69% reduction in the total number of wholesalers and distributors selling company product.

The year finished with £30m sales and a £17k profit.

How to improve the productivity of your PROCESS

-49-
Tricky conversations made easier
2022

Entire woodlands have been cut down to produce countless books on how to have affective, persuasive, engaging, tricky and difficult conversations. So, for those of you short on time here's a proven technique in under 100 words.

It's a technique I learnt in summer jobs on market stalls, serving late night drunks' fish and chips, and selling local fashionistas clothes. It's a technique which was formalised in my first *proper* job at Procter & Gamble and later refined by the highs and lows of life.

Of course, the one uncontrollable in every conversation (assuming you can control your own emotions) is the other person in the conversation, but then a conversation is meant to be shared.

Discussing with a client a potentially explosive conversation they were anxious about having with a particularly difficult member of staff who they felt was constantly undermining them, I defaulted to my own learnings and shared the following technique to make their tricky conversation easier for them - whoever said stuff like this could not be trained was wrong.

It's as simple as ABC

A. Clarify in your own mind why you need to have the conversation.

B. Identify the main purpose of the conversation, it's to achieve what?

C. Think the conversation through each of the following six phases.

1. Summarise the situation (why you are here?)
2. State the idea (what do you want?)
3. Identify the key benefit (what's so important?)
4. Explain how it works (what are the details?)
5. Summarise the benefits (what's in it for me?)
6. Agree the next steps (what do I have to do?)

Once you have completed the above preparation, set up the meeting, be mindful of the location and timings. Listen, acknowledge, answer all six questions, and most importantly share the conversation.

I can assure you that using this technique will make your tricky conversations easier.

-50-
Managing Motivational Meetings

2014

I could get far more work done if I wasn't wasting my time in so many boring meetings!

We've all heard it said and some of us, if we're honest, have thought it. It's not impossible to manage motivational meetings, so why do so many fail in what is a relatively straight forward process.

Here are ten tips on how to succeed in managing motivational meetings.

1. Start by asking yourself *"is there enough of a reason to call a meeting"* – so many automatically default to "we need a meeting".

2. Decide on the purpose of the meeting and draw up a specific agenda to meet that purpose.

3. Decide on who needs to attend and be prepared to justify your attendee list.

4. Be very clear on how long the meeting will need to be, to cover all the agenda items - do not try to cover too much in one meeting.

5. Start on time and finish on time - don't be part of the reason for the meeting over running.

6. Ensure all attendees have the opportunity to participate and contribute at the meeting.

7. Ensure that the participation and contribution is effective - be on your guard for "grenades" and don't allow yourself to be distracted from the agenda.

8. When necessary to take decisions, take decisions that are appreciated by the participants.

9. Encourage the culture that allows attendees to leave once there is nothing further for them to contribute - a simple *"does anyone have anything else for me, otherwise I'll excuse myself and get back to my desk"* usually meets with nods of approval and a thanks for your contribution.

10. Finish by summarising the commitment and get your minutes out within 48 hours with the next meeting date (if one was agreed) and agenda as the final item.

It's not impossible to manage motivational meetings.

-51-
When saying NO can enhance your brand reputation
2016

Your reputation whether personal or professional has to be protected - often from yourself as the failure or inability to say **NO** at the appropriate time and in the appropriate manner can cause lasting damage to your brand reputation.

Some people and companies just don't seem capable of saying **NO** and the alternatives of a yes or silence can result in even greater damage.

Today's apparent obsession with celebrity culture makes sound bites unchallengeable truths for many - even in business the most innocuous comments can become gospel when uttered by business guru's such as the *"say yes then learn how to do it later"* (accredited to Richard Branson) with many aspiring entrepreneurs failing to appreciate the hard work, resource, commercial know how and good fortune required to deliver the yes, which often materialises into a belated **NO** or an eerie silence.

Too many people over promise and under deliver, when all they need to do, is what they say they will do even if it's a simple *"I'm not sure but let me think about it and come back to you on Friday"*.

Saying **NO** requires a good deal of self-awareness in regard to your own, or company competencies.

If it's something you cannot do or you don't do, simply say **NO** thank you, rather than damage your reputation, you could even enhance it by referring someone who might be able to do it.

A decade or so ago, I became very concerned during a meeting with a far eastern supplier when every question I asked was met with what I later came to understand as a cultural yes.
Yes, I do have a factory, yes, I can produce that product, yes, I can meet your price, yes, you can have exclusivity, yes, I can deliver on that date. Cutting a very long and frustrating story short, the sample was delivered late, not to specification and was already being shipped into my market. Needless to say, we developed a successful and lasting relationship with another supplier.

More recently a new start-up business had received a serious enquiry from a leading Department store about their only product - the problem was the price quoted to the store was below cost.
I couldn't stress enough to the owner that they had to go back and renegotiate a price that made them a profit or simply say **NO** to the opportunity. When asked why they had quoted a price that made a loss, the owner said, *"it was too good an opportunity to miss I just had to say yes and hope to make a profit on future listings"*.

Silence is not always golden, especially when the boss has 'suggested' you arrange to meet with an external company in relation to a potential opportunity. In the world of remote offices and cyber communications these requests are usually communicated in a cover copied email to both parties.

The external company upon receipt of the introduction duly emailed the company contact to arrange a meeting and received a prompt and polite reply saying they were "busy for the next few weeks" but to call to arrange a meeting date for the following month.

A call was made along with several other calls all of which went to voice mail. Eventually the company contact answered the phone and the two managed to speak but only for a few seconds as they were "very busy", and the external contact was asked to call back the following day at 9am.

Needless to say the 9am call went to voice mail - the opportunity was missed, the company boss was *"not-very-happy"* and their employee's reputation for not being able to say "**NO** thank you it's not for us" remains legendary in their Industry.

Here's one example of how saying NO can enhance your reputation.

Hi William
I've had a chat with my production manager following our conversation yesterday and given our current commitments we don't have sufficient capacity or indeed materials to meet your requirement.
I wanted to get back to you as quickly as I could with an update to enable you to review your alternative options.
Should anything change in the next 5 weeks I will call you, in the meantime I hope you are able to find what you are looking for.
Chloe

Honesty and clarity is always appreciated, saves both parties time, manages expectations, establishes mutual respect, and enhances your brand.

-52-
Slogans Attract, Stories Engage, BUT Sales pay the Bills
2020

We like slogans, politicians, news editors and marketers especially like them because they attract attention, they are memorable and repeatable. They can be provocative or reassuring, divisive or unifying, and in the digitally obsessed world of short attention spans they rule, for example: The Rule of Six, Get Brexit Done, Build the Wall, Fake news, Every issue in Every issue, Just Do It, It's the real thing.

We love stories, no matter how old or young we are, we love a good story, and we love our story tellers. Whether that's William Shakespeare, Charles Dickens, Edin Blyton, JK Rowling, Springsteen, Christ, or Pixar. We engage with a good story and a good storyteller – it's part of our nature and adds to our sense of wellbeing, belonging and community.

There was a time all things (product, quality, service, price) being equal when you could sell something with just a slogan (name, brand, purpose), then you needed a good story as proof of slogan delivery (performance, credibility, authenticity).

The marketing campaign created to attract and engage but the ultimate purpose should be to sell more (of your) tickets, tins, cars, cans, software, services - in short to pay the bills, (and the dividends). Yet somewhere along the way it seems that the clear sales call to action (buy me) has been lost in the creativity of the storytelling or consciously air brushed out for being too vulgar.

Sales pay the bills and when the government stops paying the bills for the covid disruption to our businesses, we are going to have to work harder and smarter, to sell our products and services to pay our bills.

Converting the story into a sale (and a sale isn't a sale until the money is in the bank) often comes down to the substance of your strategy, your perception of sales, the detail of your sales plan and the skill sets of your salespeople to action the plan.

> "People don't like being sold too but they love to buy."
> Jeffrey Gitomer

The UK's largest recruitment firm Reed reported in July that job vacancies have fallen dramatically, but there had been an increase in the demand for sales professionals, suggesting companies are trying to hire their way out of the current situation.

The cheaper alternative and sometimes better solution is to train existing staff; but the focus of the training may have to change to reflect the changing needs of the market, whether that's online, in print or in person.

Accompanying sales people (just as I was when being trained and did when training others) is a great way to find out what is missing in an individual or in a process. Sadly, I am no longer surprised by how many sales people do not ask for the order.

> How fit for the future is your sales process?

-53-
How do you connect with people's emotions in an advert?

2020

This Christmas consumers want advertisers to provide festive cheer, according to research by advertising companies Unruly and Tremor Video. 47% of those surveyed want this year's Christmas ads to make them feel happy, 44% warm, 31% nostalgic, 25% inspired, 17% amused and only 15% wanted to be informed.

How do you connect with people's emotions in an advert?

You tell a story because *"People don't like being sold too but they love to buy"* (Jeffrey Gitomer) and good storytelling helps them buy-in to what's being shared, whether that's a manager aiming to secure staff "buy-in" on a change of procedure or a jewellery supplier presenting a new range to a retailer or a retail Christmas advert.

Storytelling is an art form but one that we can all learn (to varying degrees) with practice and a little help from Emma Coates. Emma used to be a Pixar Story Board Artist and has shared their 22 golden rules of storytelling. Golden because they were behind the movies that grossed over $6billion for Pixar, movies like Toy Story, Finding Nemo, The Incredibles, and Monsters Inc.

Here's my Magnificent 7 from Emma's list of 22 that I feel, easily transfer to our commercial world of pitching, presenting, and promoting.

#1: You gotta keep in mind what's interesting to you as an audience, not what's fun to do as a writer. They can be v. different.

#2: Simplify. Focus. Combine characters. Hop over detours. You'll feel like you're losing valuable stuff, but it sets you free.

#3: Come up with your ending before you figure out your middle. Seriously. Endings are hard, get yours working up front.

#4: Putting it on paper lets you start fixing it. If it stays in your head, a perfect idea, you'll never share it with anyone.

#5: Why must you tell THIS story? What's the belief burning within you that your story feeds off of? That's the heart of it.

#6: You gotta identify with your situation/characters, can't just write 'cool'. What would make YOU act that way?

#7: What's the essence of your story? Most economical telling of it? If you know that, you can build out from there.

But remember while Slogans Attract, and Stories Engage, its Sales that pay the Bills and we are going to have to work harder and smarter, to sell our products and services to pay our bills.

-54-
Company Centric Processes COST you
2017

Customer habits are changing and if you fail to anticipate them or at least follow them you will lose them. Business processes need to be customer centric; they need to serve the customer's wants; those companies that achieve this will gain business from those who don't.

Understanding your customer journey (i.e., touch points) is critical to the future of your business, customers are no longer as loyal, patient and forgiving as the older generation, today "youngsters" won't hang around, they want speed, convenience and a bonus for their effort and will move from deal to offer to deal and back again.

How customer centric are your processes?

Here are 3 ways to review your processes, from the back of an envelope to an MBA.

1. You can make your process review as simple or as detailed as you want. It doesn't have to be complicated – a lesson learnt from my Lean Six Sigma training was simply put as "walking the process" either physically, on the phone or as a cyber journey.

It can be quite startling what you see when you walk in your customers shoes, and often it's not the obvious stuff. For example, does you company organise it sales force along geographic requirements (company centric) or customer requirements?

It's a practice McDonalds have trained their managers to do once an hour every hour – leave the store and walk for 5 minutes in a different direction to the last walk, turn round and walk back this time with the eyes of the customer – what do you see that needs addressing? litter, signage, dirty windows etc.

2. Take the 5 questions DO YOU KNOW test?

> Who writes your processes?
> Who signs them off?
> When were they last reviewed?
> Are they still (externally) appropriate?
> How do they compare to your competitors' processes?

3. Here are McKinsey's recommended six actions critical to managing customer-experience journeys.

Step back and identify the nature of the journey's customers take - from the customer's point of view.

Understand how customers navigate across the touchpoints as they move through the journey.

Anticipate the customer's needs, expectations, and desires during each part of the journey.

Build an understanding of what is working and what is not.

Set priorities for the most important gaps and opportunities to improve the journey.

Come to grips with fixing root-cause issues and redesigning the journeys for a better end-to-end experience.

In recent years my credit card usage has changed not surprising really as I'm now self-employed - a coffee here, a sandwich there, and a rail ticket everywhere. Tired of entering my pin number at stations and airports for that last-minute book or snack before boarding, conscious of the commuter tuts and shuffles behind me with their contactless cards primed and ready, I decided to order a contactless credit card.

After all, how difficult could it be ...very if you bank with the "Horse Bank", as I have done for decades.

Phone Skirmish number one - approximate time 40 minutes, number of people spoken to four, outcome *"we will send you one in the post it should arrive in the next 7-10 days"*. What did arrive was a letter explaining that my type of account did not offer a contactless card!

Fast forward a few weeks and several "fuel stops" later and I decided to try again – this time requesting a contactless credit card on another of my "horse bank" account.

Phone Skirmish number two – approximate time 20 minutes, number of people spoken to two, outcome *"yes you do qualify for a contactless credit card, but we need to ask you a few questions, which should only take between 40 minutes and an hour"*.

End of conversation and a customer lost to another Bank who made it easier for me to get a contactless credit card by having customer centric KISS processes - Kept it short and sweet.

-55-
Is there a process for assessing company culture?

2019

The question was asked by an MD over dinner and discussed (at length) by the other MDs at the table - as we referenced the good, the bad and the ugly experiences we'd had. It covered vision, mission, values, and behaviours along with the cultural challenges within Multinationals, SMEs and the "Its-Just-Me" companies.

We all had opinions on what is company culture, just like you have yours.

"Organizational culture represents the collective values, beliefs and principles of organizational members and is a product of factors such as history, product, market, technology, strategy, type of employees, management style, and national culture; culture includes the organization's vision, values, norms, systems, symbols, language, assumptions, environment, location, beliefs and habits."
(Wikipedia)

But the question wasn't what is company culture? It was ...
Is there a process for assessing company culture?

Now trust me when I say every Management Consultant I've ever met, has not only an answer to that question but a model to offer you as well. Yet thanks to the internet of things, you can find your own model - that's if you have the time, and then you have to find one that will work for you, gain the support of your colleagues and one you'll be able to implement and interpret.

The ideal model is one that is workable, effective, relevant, provides employee feedback, allows for objective bench marking, is adaptable, credible, accurate and respected AND the one I always reference is The Sunday Times Best Companies to Work For - now in its 19th year!

It not only ticks all the boxes but provides a template to help you get started on assessing your own company culture.

Leadership: How employees feel about the head of the company and its senior managers.

Wellbeing: How staff feel about the stress, pressure and the balance between their work and home duties.

Giving something back: How much companies are thought by their staff to put back into society generally and the local community.

Personal growth: To what extent staff feel they are stretched and challenged by their job.

My manager: How staff feel towards their immediate boss and day-to-day managers.

My company: Feelings about the company people work for as opposed to the people they work with.

My team: How staff feel about their immediate colleagues.

Fair deal: How happy the workforce is with their pay and benefits.

        Give it a go - it might even inspire you to enter!

-56-
Ten tips on how to stop internal email undermining team spirit and limiting business growth
2013

email is a powerful business tool which can be just as damaging as it can be beneficial to a company organisation. In many companies there's too much time spent **IN** the on-screen detail and too little time spent **ON** the actual business.

A survey by McKinsey Global Institute reported office staff, spend over 25% of their time during the working day writing and responding to emails. A survey by Good Technology reported that 69% of staff check their emails before they go to bed!

Internal email culture is driven by the managers and executives of the business, it can be positive, for example by encouraging an acknowledgement of the email along with confirmation of when you'll be able to make a considered reply, or by praising an action or an outcome. It can also be negative, by its style and language, by cover copying lots of colleagues and assuming no immediate reply is an acceptance of the content. The culture is then perpetuated (or threatened) by the younger staff who have grown up in a world where texts, emails and other social media has replaced the art of verbal conversation.

Effectively squeezing those in the middle who can't beat them, so join them; and before you know it, the whole organisation is spending over 25% of their time during the working day writing and responding to emails, and some emails only travel a few metres across the office!

Here are my 5 Do and 5 Don't tips that will help you change the culture of your business and release time for you and your colleagues to spend ON the business.

Don't jump to your email notification - finish what you are doing first.

Don't BCC anyone on an internal email - avoid politics and game playing.

Don't allocate action to those you've CC and ask yourself do you really need to CC so many.

Don't type in CAPITALS or BOLD text - there's no need to SHOUT!

Don't type anything you wouldn't be prepared to say to face to face - believe in your words.

Do give consideration as to whether email is the best method for your message.

Do read through the eyes of the recipient before sending - you may wish to make a tweak.

Do set up an internal and external email box - address the latter first.

Do open your internal emails at least twice a day - if it's urgent pick up the phone.

Do delete attachments if you haven't altered them before you reply - saves time and space.

The movement of culture change can start with your own self-management of internal emails, you can: reduce the number you send; take the strain off the system; improve the verbal communication; stop the game playing; start building relationships based on trust; and release time for you and your colleagues to make a positive difference to your business.

-57-
Difficult conversations - a necessity, rarely a pleasure and all too often avoided

2015

Whether you are a Team Leader or CEO initiating difficult conversations is one of the responsibilities of your position, and one which can greatly drain not only your time but your emotions.

Yet, if handled correctly they can be very effective at turning a potentially damaging situation into a positive position, from which to change what needs to be changed.

I'm not referring to the annual appraisal, timekeeping or *the "unfortunately your promotion wasn't successful on this occasion"* conversations; but to the conversations on subjects that can get surrounded by the fog of subjectivity.

For example:
Inappropriate dress, language, behaviour; redundancy; the perceived perception of your colleagues; the lack of collective responsibility or if you're in the boardroom cabinet responsibility; and the old favourite, personal hygiene. All things which if not addressed or nipped in the bud can become distracting irritations in the business.

Here are a few tips I've used over the years to navigate my way through what I term the 5 phases of a difficult conversation.

Phase 1. The Culture
Address the reason(s) for having to have them in the first place.
Manage behaviours and expectations.

Phase 2. The Preparation
Have a very clear purpose to the conversation.
There should be no surprises in the conversation.
Check the facts.
Seek a trusted second opinion.

Phase 3. The Conversation
Be clear.
Be concise.
Be specific.
Ignore distractions.
Give first hand examples.
Listen.
Consider.
Respond, sensitively when appropriate.
Be fair, consistent and at all times professional.

Phase 4. The Outcome
Confirm your expectations.
Check their understanding.
Secure agreement on what needs to happen next.

Phase 5. The Follow Up
Provide timely feedback both positive and negative but always constructive.

-58-
The Good, the Bad and the Ugly Redundancies

2020

Firms planning 20 or more redundancies at a single "establishment" must by law notify the government via a form called HR1, of how many people they are potentially making redundant.

On September 8th, the BBC released HR1 figures, secured via a Freedom of Information request that revealed a six-fold increase in plans to cut jobs in June 2020 compared to June 2019, and a seven-fold increase in July on the previous July. But that wasn't particularly surprising nor was the headline that 38% of firms in the private sector compared to 16% in the public sector planned to make redundancies, as reported in research by the Chartered Institute of Personnel and Development (CIPD) and recruiter Adecco.

But when the folds and percentages are converted to affected individuals, close to half a million redundancies are likely to be announced in the autumn, although the number could end up exceeding 700,000, according to a study by the Institute for Employment Studies; and that's on top of 240,000 redundancies officially recorded by the government up until June.

One million people could be made redundant in 2020.

Companies making cost savings to address their business performance in the context of decimated revenues and recovery models is responsible management, but that's not the news story on this blog page nor is the story of those potentially guilty of addressing long standing previously ignored business issues by the opportunity presented by covid19.

No, this blog is to encourage more of the good redundancy practices and less of the bad and downright ugly!

British Airways has been accused of *"appalling behaviour that puts a Victorian mill owner to shame"* in its treatment of staff. (Independent). Some British Airways staff who have accepted voluntary redundancy say they had felt 'forced' into it. Carol (not her real name) said of her BA experience *"Even before I had accepted the voluntary redundancy offer, I had a message on my roster from BA: 'Thank you for your service. Good luck'. That is all I got from them after 23 years"*. (BBC News)

During August I caught up with 3 people who had sadly lost their jobs due to pandemic restructuring and I heard 3 very, different personal stories.

The Good - the Sales Director - sales during C19 dropped from $50m a month to $5m a month (yep I thought I'd misheard too) *"they made me a very good offer, very early on and I took it"*.

The Bad - the Regional Director - a complete lack of detail, more U turns than the government and an apparent disregard for the legal process.

The Ugly - the CEO - having to deal with an external consultant who had all the finesse of Donald Trump.

Having been on both sides of the redundancy table I decided to balance things up and hosted a zoom group of 6 SME Owners who were in one of the following 3 stages of redundancy: completed the process, in the process of completing or considering the process.

Here's their advice for other owners, to ensure a good redundancy process:

1. Start with a full business review and use that to drive your decision.
2. Resist the temptation to take short cuts.
3. Consult with a HR professional before, during and after.
4. Regular staff engagement will help avoid any nasty surprises.
5. Double check everyone has received ALL the information.
6. Listen to all staff ideas, proposals, suggestions and respond to all, logically and calmly.
7. Avoid being reactive, be proactive in thought, speech, and action.
8. Be present at the meetings.
9. Don't underestimate the emotional impact on individuals.
10. Stick to your guns if you believe in the decision.

10 plus years ago I found myself in a city I'd only previously visited once before and standing in a queue recognised a former colleague with a rather BIG husband at her side (the big is relevant).

The conversation went something like this ...

Me... *"Hi Susan, how are you? It's Michael Donaldson"*
Susan... vague look on her face, then she places me, *"I remember you; you made me redundant!"*
Me... awkward and now very conscious of the size of her husband who was staring at me, along with others in the queue ... *"am sure I did it nicely"*.
Susan... *"yes you did, how are you? What brings you here?"*

"I've learned that people will forget what you said that people will forget what you did, but people will never forget how you made them feel". Maya Agelou

-59-
Many appointments fail because of a poor interview/er
2023

You've written the job description, the essential and desirable lists, a brilliant advert, fantastic candidate questions, and have set aside time in the diary to interview the chosen few. What could possibly go wrong now – apart from the interviewee not turning up and interviewer using the wrong selection criteria.

I recently completed a survey of some 30 plus SME business owners, which suggested most appointments are made on emotions and first impressions, rather than the answers to behavioural and competency questions.

48% of those surveyed were driven by emotion and feelings, (we are people after all) looking for a *"vibe in the room, a fit with my small team, a sense of humour, punctuality, appearance, eye contact, and availability"*.

20% selected candidates on *"conversational skills, approachability, common sense and what they can bring to the team."*

32% took all of the above into account, along with scored answers to specific questions against a pre-defined, easy to apply definition of what constitutes a poor or good answer.

The wrong approach and the wrong selection criteria have (and will continue to) put the wrong people, in the wrong jobs, in the wrong

companies - resulting in everyone involved, wasting time, money, energy and sleep, before returning back to where they started 3, 6 or 9 months earlier facing another round of interviews.
Thinking of my best and worst interviews.

My best interview must be my first career interview which took place during the university *milk round* nothing to do with delivering milk, but the term used to describe the best companies coming on campus to milk the best candidates before they had even sat their finals. I was so relaxed having never really been interviewed before and felt very little pressure as this job was nothing more than an access to a car and free weekends.
(I'd already decided that leisure experiences were going to be massive in the UK and I planned to own an Outdoor Pursuits Centre, the first step to which was gaining some outdoor pursuits experience and was already in possession of a deferred place on one of only two programmes in the UK that trained in all things OP - mountaineering, caving, climbing, camping, hiking, sailing, skiing).

So, I felt no pressure and what they saw and got, was me. A second interview followed, followed by lunch, and I'd received a job offer 8 months before I'd even graduated.

I've since read the company I joined for the car and the weekends reject 97% of applicants - that's another reason I believe in miracles *(six months after starting work I'd not had time to climb a single peak over 2,000 feet let alone the 20 I'd been tasked with, but I loved the job and released my held place for someone who really wanted a career in OPCs).*

The interview takeaways are RELAX and be YOURSELF.

Which can be difficult in this cyber age of video pitches, zoom interviews, screen tests, assessment centres, psychometric testing, team building exercises, seven stage interview processes and that's just for the graduate starters.

The discussion consensus amongst the SME owners was an ideal mix of scoring and gut. I once heard Janet Street-Porter, describe this as a dinner party test. *"Could I sit next to this person for three hours over dinner? If the answer is yes, I knew I could work with them."*

HOWEVER, and there's always a HOWEVER, there needs to be an increased sensitivity to and a safeguard against, potential claims of discrimination in the interview or the interview process. Some in the room believed there needed to be two interviewers in the room, both making their own notes, the questions need to be the same if asked a little differently in the conversation to illicit the response on the same said topic. On the upside, the notes, and questions (which had to be held by you for 12 months) also enable you to assess candidates fairly against the job role and other candidates, as well as reference meaningful feedback. At which point, I default to my usual recommendation of *"refer to your HR specialist for guidance before acting"* on this discussion.

Which is just what I did by calling Tarnya Brink (FCIPD) at Invictus HR and asked her firstly about the GDPR implications:

"The Data Protection Act 2018 controls how personal data is used and one of the requirements is that data is only retained for as long as is necessary. Ideally companies will have a Data Protection Policy and Retention guide which sets out how information is used and how long different aspects of personal data is retained."

Secondly, do the interview documents really have to be held for 12 months?

"As a rule, we recommend that recruitment documents (CV, Application, Interview Notes) are kept for 6 months, or longer if you have specific permission from the applicant to retain their documents for longer, e.g. if you know you are likely to recruit for the same position again within a relatively short period. A 6-month retention period means that if there is a challenge on the grounds of discrimination for a protected characteristic, which they have 3 months less one day days to submit to ACAS, you have the evidence to support the decision you made."

Once you have your questions, check that they are job role and job requirement related, and focused on understanding how the candidates experience fulfils the role.

For candidate comparison purposes, you'll need a score card for each candidates' answers – Below is one I created 20 years ago which seems to be just as relevant today.

Initial answer to the question plus any examples of related experience

5 Very Good - with more than 1 related example.
4 Good - with a related example.
3 Standard - with standard examples.
2 Lacking - with unrelated examples.
1 Poor - with no examples.

It doesn't have to be complicated, it doesn't need 10 scores, or long definition sentences; the more you're writing the less you are listening to and looking at the person in front of you.

And my worst interview.

There was a time when the recruitment agency would fill your diary with their shortlisted candidates, for you to spend all day in a hotel room asking 7 or 8 different hopefuls the same questions one after another. Notetaking was critical because I can assure you by 3pm, it's all becoming a blur and it was always the 4pm candidate that cancelled and you had to wait in the hope the five o'clock would turn up, before you could head home after the days debrief at 6.30pm.

If it was a role that required driving, my checklist always included a note to check their driving licence, on this particular day, a preferred candidate had forgotten to bring it with him. At the second he'd forgotten it because he'd *just buried his father.* At the end of his first day, he met my boss's boss for a handshake and chat. Handshakes all round, I was reminded to get a copy of his driving licence which I duly did before waving him off in his new car, with sales samples, fuel card and cash float.

On the way home I called in at a police station and asked them to interpret the coding and letters on his paper licence - in short, he had served a ban and was close to serving a second ban!

The following day he phoned in sick.

I took the news to my Boss who took me and the news to his Boss, which in its self was a lesson. Between them they very quickly agreed the following plan. My role was to look, listen, and learn. The three of us drove to our new employee's home. I sat in the car and waited for my Boss and his Boss to return with the keys to his car, company documentation, selling samples and what remained of his cash float.

I drove back on my own, in the recovered car giving me plenty of time to reflect on the lesson learned, and never repeated.

-60-
10 Reasons why Appraisals FAIL
2017

In 2015 a survey of senior business leaders by the Chartered Institute of Personnel and Development on attitudes to appraisals reported that 73% of leaders considered annual appraisals ineffective.

John Timpson in his book Upside Down Management reveals that *"we abandoned appraisals 25 years ago and have survived happily ever since"* they were replaced with a culture *"where everyone can raise problems and talk about their future with their Boss"* and one assumes vice versa – the Boss can have similar conversations with their staff.

Appraisals are found in all sorts of situations:
The act of assessing something or someone – such as a house survey.

Impartial analysis and evaluation conducted according to established criteria to determine the acceptability, merit, or worth of an item – such as a jewellery valuation.

A meeting in which an employee discusses their progress, aims, and needs at work with their manager or employer – simply put as a conversation.

My own straw poll of a dozen SME business owners revealed that only 25% do appraisals, 17% have allowed them to lapse and over half of them have never done an appraisal.

Alarmingly but not surprisingly some of the reasons given for not doing an appraisal are conversation related – not wanting to upset people; avoiding confrontation and not wanting to open a can of worms.

My first appraisal took place once a year between me and my manager and was a handwritten performance review of six factors essential to effective performance in my role, and from memory lasted the best part of half a day. Fast forward 30 years and my appraisals were quarterly between me and my CEO and lasted no more than an hour. There was a time in between when I was being appraised online, on 22 job relevant competencies by 13 colleagues whose feedback was anonymous.

A quick calculation on the back of an envelope suggests that during my time as a company employee I received over 60 appraisals and conducted over 675 - some were good, some were not so good, and only a few were memorable.

Conducting an effective appraisal requires demanding personal skills such as the ability to listen, show empathy, think objectively, and communicate clearly. Though appraisals in my experience often fail for simpler reasons, than a skills deficiency – below are 10 of them.

1. Too long or too short
2. Infrequent
3. No feedback
4. Fixation with weaknesses
5. Personal bias (positive as well as negative)
6. Inconsistent standards
7. Poor scoring criteria
8. Unachievable objectives
9. Appraising irrelevancies
10. Avoid your office – use a neutral venue, as it creates a more relaxed atmosphere for your conversation.

-61-
Promotion should be a piece of PIE

2016

Whether you're making the appointment, seeking the appointment or in the early stages of succession planning for the appointment, there are 3 basic ingredients that you need in your recipe for success: Performance Image and Exposure (PIE).

The term PIE came to prominence two decades ago in a book by Harvey Coleman called Empowering Yourself: The Organizational Game Revealed, which in summary says there is a lot more to getting promoted than working hard and being in the right place at the right time - it's more about image and exposure and less about performance.

Traditionally believed to be 60% performance 30% image and 10% exposure, many Coaches and HR specialists today would flip those percentages round with 60% on exposure. For if the people who matter, (the decision makers and influencers) don't know who you are and what you are capable of, the odds are against you before you have even put finger to keyboard.

Performance is a given - You differentiate yourself from your peers not only through a superior performance, a given for all promotional candidates but with a better image and a wider exposure. I'm not referring to social media pages, which at times have been known to be more damaging to an application than supportive; and should be managed responsibly and maturely.

If performance is a given, then the differentiators are behaviours and attitudes that in turn form and shape your public image and exposure.

Image is critical - it's what people immediately think of when they hear your name. It's your reputation, style, interaction, and your manner of doing things, in today's parlance your personal brand.

I've been at meeting tables when manager A shares their plans for person B to be appointed to position C and the responses in the room have been illustrative of how quickly we label people we don't particularly know very well and allow those labels to form and shape our perceptions. Consider the connotations of these throw away labels: *"a safe pair of hands", "lacks gravitas", "it's too soon", "doesn't see the big picture", "I wouldn't like to sit next to them on a long flight".* Labels can and do influence decisions - its human nature.

Exposure is critical - its which people are able to immediately think of you (positively) when they hear your name, in today's parlance your personal network. Exposure acts as the catalyst for your Image and Performance and can make all the difference - there's still a lot of truth in the English proverb "it's not what you know but who you know."

Coleman tells a story about sheltering from a snowstorm during which he recognises a senior executive from his company is in the same shelter – he strikes up a conversation that lasts the best part of the storm and the two, part to continue their skiing. Six months later he is fast tracked for a promotion. Get that conversation wrong and the wrong image can get you the wrong exposure and it could well be your own job you're reapplying for in the next restructure – as I found out to my cost when a 30-minute site tour with the Group CEO extended to 3 hour discussion. During which my usually respectful, considered self, gave way to a *'tell them how it is'* fuelled by prescribed steroids (aka truth drug) for a very nasty virus I'd picked up in the Far East.

Another time, I remember being one of a number of managers called in to present our business to the management team that had just acquired our business; standard stuff really, who what why how etc. What surprised me was the difference in the questioning techniques used by the incoming directors. I had a relatively easy time; one or two others were less fortunate and didn't make the end of the week.

Sometime later I discovered the incoming management had spoken to my network of customers as part of their due diligence and the decision to retain me had effectively been made before I'd even stood up to present.

Succession Planning - stress the importance of image and exposure to everyone you're positioning or sponsoring for promotion, ensure they understand that whilst you know what a great person, they are others don't. Ensure they understand how important their attitudes and behaviours are in shaping and forming their image and exposure. That they need to consistently perform in their meetings, in their communications, in managing their people and their interaction with other teams - because people form impressions on what they see and hear.

5 Tips on PIE making:

1. Accept that superior performance is a given and must be a consistent ingredient.

2. Turn up the temperature on occasions to secure the labels that will promote your appeal.

3. Do not rush your networking - the best advocate networks require time to rise.

4. Seek out PIE makers and observe their baking techniques.

5. Be authentic otherwise you'll be exhausted trying to be someone you're not.

-62-
Secrets of Success and Succession
2021

Your individual definition of what success is will vary according to the context, whether it is personal or professional, business, or social.

What's success for one business may be failure for another business, depending on the criteria you set at the start to help you recognise what success will look like. For some organisations being able to reopen the doors after the pandemic was success, for others supporting and retaining staff through the lockdown was success, for others generating revenue from a new digital platform was success and for others completing a new acquisition was success. It is all relative!

Success doesn't just happen, it comes from planning, resourcing, and implementation; and all that entails in terms of time and commitment - though a little bit of luck is always welcomed. It all starts with the plan, because a goal without a plan is just a wish; and the success of the plan is very dependent on implementing its detail. A small retailer shared with me how they had made a little tweak to a successful promotion last run 4 years ago - a tiny detail, something as simple as a handwritten address had helped them generate an additional £51,000 sales.

Whether you are a family run SME, a large National or the $650billion Berkshire Hathaway looking to appoint a successor to the 90-year-old Warren Buffet, be very clear on what the role requires to not only survive but thrive in the future.

Succession planning requires vision, knowledge, and patience, which doesn't come overnight but can stop you making the wrong appointment that will give you sleepless nights.

Work life emotions, practices, and satisfaction has probably changed more in the last 18 months than they have in the last 18 years and the requirements looked for in a new leader for your business needs to reflect that. It's less of the same old, same old, and more of the same, same, but different.

Similarly, family members being promoted in haste, at times beyond their capabilities, without the infrastructure, support, or investment to survive and thrive can give everyone sleepless nights including employees and retired owners.

The actual handover process is key - too quick and there will be knowledge gaps, too long and there could be confusion and frustration. It's good practice when handing over, to have each responsibility explained and trained (for one final time) before giver and receiver both sign off against each responsibility as completed and accepted.

A process that helps you work back from the planned exit date of the giver to ensure the receiver gets sufficient time to oversee a seamless transition for all stakeholders – customers, suppliers, employees, bank manager, and soon to be retired owners.

But it all starts with planning the plan.

-63-
Seven questions every Board needs to answer ASAP

2020

Even high performing, strategically sound businesses, that have been run extremely well over the pre-covid years, are having to reassess their futures. Some will become stronger, some will recover, and some will cease, but there is one thing for certain, not everything will return to normal once this pandemic is beaten.

The 7P questions a board should be addressing to understand the business realities of the country coming out of lockdown.

Q1. Power Struggles?
The normal world order is in the process of being tipped upside down as the economic superpowers vie for supremacy. The established organisations and bodies that have framed our current global relationships such as the EU, WHO, WTO, NATO, UN, even UNESCO are all being challenged or undermined or simply ignored.

25 years ago, China's economy was smaller than Spain's economy, today it is the second largest in the world behind the US. It is already home to 28% of the world's manufacturing, nearly as much as the US, Germany and Japan combined. The country is our third largest trading partner after the US and EU; and has been busy funding "overseas" investment, securing economic and political influence, and now has significant representation in over 70 countries around the globe.

So, what has that got to do with your business?

Nothing unless you, your suppliers and your customers are insulated from changes in international trade tariffs, exchange rates, product compliance, innovation etc – imagine the conversations that have taken place in the UK Boardrooms of the companies involved with the 5G roll out and all that means to the future shape and size of our economy.

Q2. Potential Opportunities?
Acting now could position a business not only to survive covid19 but prosper post covid19.

Market share will be available from the failure of competitor businesses to re-open or stay open but more immediately for those businesses who handle the crisis better than others, from simple PPE measures to sensitive and clear communications.

Acquisition targets will be cheaper, and more acquisition opportunities (be they companies, people, products, or processes), will present themselves as businesses struggle to recover.

Cash has never been so cheap, so now's the time to be reviewing if you have sufficient cash or the investment means to support growth through acquisition, new product development or process innovation.

Q3. Purpose?
One thing that probably hasn't changed for the majority, is a company's purpose - the why a company does what it does.

That's not to say it hasn't or won't be affected by accelerated changes in how we think and feel about the issues and opportunities facing us as we continue to address life in and beyond this pandemic.

After months in social isolation, waiting for life to reboot and worrying about what the future may bring; many more people will be looking for more meaningful work and as we all know, those engaged with a strategic purpose generally contribute more to a business - as every B Corporation business will testify too!

Actions are now expected on the pre-pandemic issues round diversity, inclusion, equal pay, climate change and BLM. Company words and good intentions will no longer cut it with the pandemic public - the mood has changed.

Q4. People?
As some of the 9 million UK furloughed workers begin to return to work, it'll be an emotional and anxious time for some and a different return for all; beginning with the commute, compounded by a work environment that demands distancing, PPE, and possibly different start and finish times. One of the challenges facing businesses will be resetting their culture (and policies) with employees potentially working at home, in the office, in the warehouse or in the call centre. How quickly they can re-establish a sense of common purpose, shared identity and a sense of belonging will give them an advantage.

The return to work will carry a huge cost for both business and state and will likely impact on disposable household incomes and the recovery of our economies.

The mental, emotional, and physical states of those returning to work will need support and patience. Speaking to recently re-opened retailers they have already received requests for: holidays, a pay rise to cover increased commute costs, shorter hours, extended furlough due to lack of child care and a member of staff who had "other" plans for the following week didn't want to come back in. A friend had his office relocated from Canary Wharf to Acton, and his week will now be spent between there and home – he's not happy, especially with the additional commute time and the further intrusion of work on his home life.

Others will be fearful of redundancies as furlough support ends and businesses have insufficient sales or reserves to maintain them before revenues return to anywhere near normal.
This type of change and uncertainty could lead to high performers looking elsewhere for increased security in expanding and pandemic proof sectors. On the flip side companies may find they have a greater choice of who they hire than in times of low unemployment.

Q5. Product?
Internal discussion will be driven by how companies regard their products / services but more importantly how their customers regard them; to use pandemic parlance – are you supplying non-essential or essentials?

As a profit rule it's always better to choose difference over discount and to avoid responding in kind to product dumping and price cutting, which is easier if your products have a compelling difference.

Businesses supplying the retail sector may find they have fewer customers than they had pre-lockdown because of high street closures. Others face with being exposed by a reduced customer base and will need to find new customers ideally with higher margin business. Others who responded to the call to provide home deliveries, PPE, ventilators, vaccines, online services and the like, may well find they now have an a new product line, and new relationships in new sectors which they are well placed to grow and develop alongside their existing business.

Q6. Process?
The pandemic impact on processes will present opportunities and threats across the business, here are just a few examples to kick start your discussions:

Innovation - acceptance has accelerated from Zoom to Drones, the latter have been used in the pandemic to spray slums in Mexico, deliver meals in California, mail in France and medicines in Rwanda.

Shipping Delays - the majority of goods still travel on cargo ships but with ports closed around the globe very little is actually being delivered and lead times are no longer being quoted. In June 250,000 mariners were stranded on ships anchored outside ports and another 250,000 were sitting at home not knowing when they'd next be contracted – that's a significant percentage of the 1.2 million mariners that keep our goods moving.

Resourcing and Onshoring - countries and factories not yet open or recently re-opened or re-closed in a new outbreak, are struggling to fund orders and deliveries.

Supply Shortages - have led companies to address their supply chains. A recent USP survey of 1000 big companies reported that 76% of firms from America 85% from North Asia and even 60% from China say they have already moved or plan to move some production away from China.

Online Shopping - is no longer the domain of food, clothes, books, music, and small ticket items. 4 months of lockdown has introduced millions to the convenience (and security) of online shopping; perceptions and habits have changed as have the price tickets.

Sales Skills - the UK's largest recruitment firm Reed has reported that job vacancies have fallen dramatically, but there has been an increase in the demand for sales professionals. How fit for the future is your sales process?

Finance - the cost of money has never been so cheap in terms of interest rates, but it may prove more difficult and ultimately more costly getting your hands on it, as lenders are increasingly risk averse. Then there is the cost of trade credit insurance against unpaid invoices, the impact on cash flow, the impact of credit ratings, and the impact of the currency markets. The business also needs to understand the risk – in terms of who owes who and how much, where are the biggest sector, customer and supplier exposures and ultimately how long will the cash last.

The Next Pandemic - what lessons have been learnt in during covid 19, that will help the business mitigate the damage of the next pandemic.

Q7. Profit?
Just one question that needs answering here, how will the above impact the profit line?

Some will become stronger; some will recover, and some will cease, but there is one thing for certain, not everything will return to normal once this pandemic is beaten.

-64-
Acceptable is NOT Acceptable
2022

How would you like to have your business described as acceptable - is there anything worse?

It's so... okay, average, fine, alright, and worryingly neutral. It's a feeling that does not excite or is ever likely to retain a customer let alone make them an advocate for your business.

I've been working with an award-winning business which missed out on the medals this year due to an *acceptable* rating of their customer service, the owner was furious, not for missing out but for having their business described as "acceptable".

Their initial reaction questioned the objectivity of the "mystery shopper", failing perhaps to remember that most high street shoppers and many B2B purchasers are extremely subjective when it comes to making a buying decision. After a bad night's sleep, they reconsidered the feedback in the context of what could help them improve the customer perception of their business, because as we know, perception is FACT.

I can't remember ever working in a business, or on a board or in a team or with individuals who just wanted to do an acceptable job - can you?

When have you ever: appointed someone with an attitude of acceptable being acceptable; joined a business that didn't want to be good at what it did; or started a business with the mission of being acceptable?

In my experience successful businesses, organisations, and individuals are those that believe that "Acceptable is NOT Acceptable".
Yet so many businesses today, seem to accept the acceptable - poor service, poor quality, late deliveries, out of stocks, unannounced door step drops, substitute products, standing room only, untrained staff and the unacceptable on hold loop message ... *"we are receiving particularly high levels of calls at the moment, your call is important to us and we will get to you as soon as possible or you could just push-off to our website blah blah"*.

10 months ago, my wife and I made a trip to our local kitchen appliance retailer, following a number of excellent recommendations from satisfied neighbours. Sadly, the local retailer was unable to confirm the price or delivery of the appliances we selected from the international brand Neff; allegedly due to Brexit and Covid (really??).
The new (higher) price followed a week later but the delivery date remained an unknown, so we decided to postpone our purchase for 3 months to see if the situation improved in the new year. The stock situation did not improve, the lead time was now 10-16 weeks and the price had gone up again ... so we paid the deposit to secure the price and decided to wait.

On week 12, I contacted the retailer for an update to be told that they *"cannot give me any schedule or time scale ... as there was a delay due to a worldwide component shortage for the displays in the oven and microwave combi which come from Ukraine so unfortunately their hands are tied"*.

10 months on and what frustrated me most was the lack of proactive communication, the whiff of BS when they did communicate and the attitude *"it's not our fault"* – acceptable you may think given the impact

of the Brexit decision (6 years ago?), Covid 19 (2 years ago?) and I'm not totally convinced the latest delay is down to the war in Ukraine - because Neff's website reassuringly says *"we have production sites in 38 countries, so we are not as constricted as some and can manage production a little easier."* I think both these businesses were guilty of accepting the acceptable. *(It took 14 months to get the appliances delivered and fitted!)*

Whilst writing this, I picked up on a comment made by a frustrated owner of a B2C business after a particularly difficult day... *"remember the days after the pandemic and everyone was patient and wouldn't mind how long things took? Those days are long gone it seems!!"* And they are long gone, with lockdowns, shortages, and "Putinflation", people now want immediate gratification - they want to pick, pay, and take their purchase away, along with memories of a hassle-free enjoyable transaction.

What can you do to make your business stand out in the landscape of acceptability?

How can you not only retain but attract new customers?

What do you have to do to make your customers advocates for your business?

For those who are in non-customer facing roles, the same applies for you, as you look to stand out, have colleagues say good things about you, attract a promotion, and earn a salary increase.

Transitioning perceptions from neutral to positive doesn't have to be complicated, it's about embedding a culture where *"acceptable is not acceptable"*, which starts very logically by ensuring you and your people are *"Brilliant at the Basics"*.

How highly would you score your business in these 10 everyday basics?
1. Not at all 2. Not very 3. Acceptable 4. Very highly 5. Extremely highly

Establishing a rapport.
Listening.
Asking relevant questions.
Understanding requirements.
Providing relevant and requested information.
Being transparent and honest about situations.
Managing expectations.
Taking complaints seriously.
Giving due attention to the detail.
And being human not a bot!
All very BASIC, so if you struggle doing them don't be surprised if you lose customers.

I recently selected a beautiful, *hand-picked* hotel that I've used many times for meetings and dinners, to celebrate my wedding anniversary, ensuring my contact at the hotel knew it was a personal occasion not a business gathering. As we drove home after a wonderful meal with a lovely personal touch or two, I mused on what had been slightly disappointing – having to find our own way from the bar to the restaurant as our seating time came and went, having to share a menu because they had run out, attempting to clear the table whilst Mrs D was still eating, the noise setting the tables for breakfast and the wait to get the bill – basics! My musings being interrupted by my wife's voice *"don't worry about it, the food was fabulous but if you want the service you have to go to a restaurant not a hotel because that's where restaurants excel, it's their business"*. Note-to-self, remember to book a restaurant for next year's anniversary!

The last score you want as a business, organisation or individual is acceptable - it's just NOT acceptable!

-65-
How to Navigate Wage Inflation

2022

Six months ago, staff wage issues were centred around the impact of covid and the great resignation as SMEs increased salaries to attract and retain staff – with two business owners telling me at the time that they had to pay 5 figure increases to retain a key retail staff member and the other a vital PA; increases that would normally have taken at least five years to achieve.

But as we all know the world has changed and changed again ... first we had Brexit, then Covid, and now War further increasing the cost of living for your staff on basic items like cooking oil, bread, and essential items like fuel, gas, and electricity – with further heating hikes to come in the next 6 months.

And there's little comfort for business owners knowing that most of the advanced economies in the world are facing predicted rises in inflation at levels not seen for decades – that's far too remote for those currently contemplating a second or third increase in their wage bill in the last 9 months.

Wage inflation will hit your bottom-line FACT by how much depends on what you do to protect your bottom line and more importantly your people. That's if your business depends on people and you adopt the mantra that business is all about people and you acknowledge that your business is only as good as your people. Then your people must be insulated at the very least from these inflationary pressures.

Obvious insulation can come from - repositioning your own pricing, restructuring your delivery options, developing new products, enhancements, or specification changes. Increased automation to save time and release time for greater value add activities not just to cut jobs, shortening supply chains by shopping local, and letting go of unprofitable lines no matter how attached you are to them. In short, a root and branch review of your People Product Process.

All of which helps but it doesn't help staff with today's heating bills. That will require all your emotional intelligence not just hard facts and numbers to ensure you secure both customer and staff relationships for the longer term once this external pressure has subsided or at least is more controllable within your business.

"We just gave every F/T member of staff a £1,000 bonus, pro rata for part timers. It was an extra top up over the Christmas bonus based on last year's profits rather than being based on fuel increases etc, but increased cost of living was a consideration in the timing."
Manufacturing MD

"We gave an inflationary increase to all staff in September last year averaging 10%. This was the first increase for 2.5 years. We worked out through RPI change we would have had to give at least a 6% rise to ensure their wages matched 2.5 years ago. We increased it to 10% as a reward for loyalty and incentivize staff to stay. Looking at RPI now we would have to give a 10% rise to match 3 years ago so the extra 4% we gave in September for loyalty has already been eroded. Hence, we will probably need to give a 3-4% rise this month in order to maintain the value of staff's wages." Retail Business Owner

Wages and benefits are one of an SMEs biggest cost and in today's inflationary climate one of the biggest draws for new recruits BUT do not underestimate the attraction of an attractive culture that allows an employee to restore some post covid work life balance... Afterall you can't keep signing off salary increases every six months or so.

"In one financial services company, leaders increased salary ranges by 15 percent to try to keep employees from leaving, but attrition levels stayed the same. That's because the company had not addressed concerns about untenable hours and high-pressure assignments, nor had it acknowledged the churn going on within the industry...To rebuild relationships and retain current employees while attracting new ones, CEOs must guide their companies to take a new approach to talent."
McKinsey

At the start of the year, I was supporting my client businesses with a framework on how to deal with supplier price increases – a framework, that with a little license, can now be applied to navigating the current round of wage inflation affecting SME businesses.

10 Navigation Pointers for Wage Inflation:

1. Understand the impact on your team of applying the wage increase.

2. Prioritise your exposure on your key people within the business - losing key people can create unintended consequences, such as negative customer perceptions & lost sales.

3. Understand which jobs are facing the greatest wage inflation.

4. Remember the media headline inflation costs do not apply to or affect everyone or every sector the same way - get to understand individual pain points.

5. Leverage your staff relationships, by keeping your dialogue honest and transparent - this will help minimise staff resignations and strengthen the bonds between you.

6. Offer carefully designed performance incentives to retain and reward staff.

7. Give wage increases only when you are fully aware of their impact on your bottom line.

8. Seek win win payments.

9. Losing key staff for the sake of a principle or a double-digit percentage increase could well cost you more in recruiting a replacement.

10. Wage inflation will hit your bottom-line FACT – by how much depends on what you do to protect your bottom line and more importantly your people.

In summary

Don't just accept it without doing your homework.
Have the conversation with the staff.
Consider the alternatives.
Be decisive and move on.

-66-
Are you spending enough time ON your business to deliver real Growth?
2015

As the senior manager in your business, you are responsible for setting the future direction of the business and your people are depending on you to make the right decisions. These decisions cannot be taken effectively, without spending sufficient time ON the business.

Working ON the business means ensuring you have the people, products, and processes in place to deliver your growth strategy.

Working IN the business means that your people, products, and processes are all performing effectively to achieve the growth strategy.

Let us assume for the sake of these 2 quick exercises that you work a 5-day week in a 52-week year, giving you a 260-day year. That you take a total of 6 weeks "off" for personal and public holidays, so now your year is now closer to 230 days than 365 days.

Let us now assume that you spend just 1 day a week in meetings, that's 46 days, just 1 day a week managing your email inbox, and just 1 day a week following up on your meeting and email actions that's another 92 days – Over 60% of the working year gone and you've not yet had any (real) time ON the business.

Exercise #1
Look back through your diary for the last month and quickly jot down how much time you spent ON the business – time away from the day to day, to think, discuss or plan the future of your business?

Include the time you spent in specific planning meetings, or reading, networking, attending conferences, meeting with your customers, stakeholders or with your external peer group.
Total it up and express it as a % of your working month...
If you scored less than 5% ... you are not even thinking about growth
If you scored between 5 % and 10% ... you are not serious about real growth. So, what's stopping you spending more time ON the business?

Exercise#2
Look back through your diary for the last quarter and identify what you did with your time?
When I did this in my role as a Commercial Director it roughly fell into 3 equally split areas: external meetings, internal meetings, and desk time (not really surprising given my role). Drilling down into each of the areas, I was able to identify the IN the business and the ON the business activity and shift the balance accordingly for the benefit of myself, my team, and my business. How much time you spend ON the business, depends on what your growth plans are ... for example a merger or acquisition could demand greater ON time than a new product or service; a new market entry could demand greater ON time than a new site opening.

Size is NOT an excuse.
I often hear small business owners (who wear many hats), say that they simply don't have the time to step back from / out of / let go of the business as they find themselves fighting fires, placating dissatisfied customers, getting the website back up and tidying the books for the accountant's visit tomorrow. But if their primary reasons for doing things themselves is to save money, or that they feel they can do it much faster and better than anyone else in the business, they should think of the opportunity cost. As business owners they set the direction and growth goals of the business and they have a greater chance of success, the more time they spend time ON the business. If you are still struggling to find more ON time then try starting with just one hour a day, spent on planning the implementation of an idea you heard about or read about or saw in action - it can be as small and as simple as you like, as long as you think it will add value to your business.

-67-
How to realise data Value from data Usage

2021

I was recently on a zoom panel at the World Jewellery Confederation* 2021 Congress - it was the final global open session, and the digital audience was truly global but down 60% on the open session average. Not that I took it personally you understand – the topic *Dealing with Data in the Digital world (sic)* sadly doesn't seem to rock (pun intended) many business owners' boats, which in my mind is BONKERS as data can be gold dust if used correctly or just dust if ignored.

But I would say that, as I was baptised in the value of data whilst working at P&G in the FMCG sector and when at Williams Holdings in the SDA sector I was investing tens of thousands in GfK epos data, and I wasn't on my own. Suppliers bought data, retailers bought data, analysts bought data, and they all used it to guide their decisions and grow their business, such was and still is the importance of data.

 * CIBJO est. in 1926 has members in over 40 countries and represents the entire industry from mine to marketplace. In 2006 it received official consultative status with ECOSOC of the United Nations.

My time in these sectors taught me two key data lessons:
1. An opinion without data is just an opinion.
2. Whether it's BIG data or small data, if you don't use it - it's just data.

As an SME, you may see purchasing data as an unnecessary expense or you don't have the budget for data or you might be operating in a GfK data free sector, or you believe that data can't make a positive difference to your business performance.

Yet there's lots of free data out there, some is usable, some is informative, the majority just opinion but combined it provides food for thought and planning your business decisions over the next few years will require a lot of thought in the absence of a crystal ball.

A good starting point are trade magazines, trade associations, press articles, and reports published by your local Chamber of Commerce, or IoD branch; all of which can be sense checked with your internal colleagues or external networks.

If you're too busy to spend time searching for external data, then start with your own internal data that focuses on your business pain points. Quick wins in these areas builds confidence and increases the appetite for using more data to drive business improvement activities. It doesn't have to be complicated, so keep it simple to begin with and avoid over complicating the process. For example, managing millions of pounds of stock starts with 3 questions - the answers to which can improve your performance in stock turn, cash flow and buying process.

1. What % of your stock sells in the same year you put it into stock?
2. What % of your stock sells in the year after you put it into stock?
3. What % of your stock is three or more years old and growing a beard sitting in stock?

But it should not all be about time, and cost, there are also indirect benefits that come with data usage such as increased objectivity, accountability, appreciation, clarity, communication, teamwork, and problem solving - everything business leaders strive to instil in their people.

If you've never used data or have stopped using data, here's a dozen snippets on collecting and using data, to help you improve the performance of your business.

1. Just get started because the important thing about getting started is, just getting started.

2. Do more with what you've got but remember Rubbish in means Rubbish out.

3. If you haven't got a system that collects the data, you need to GET ONE.

4. Use data that will quickly address your current pain points.

5. Know what you want from the data and define it in terms of clear key performance indicators – start with a handful at first.

6. Know how you want to manipulate the data, to be able to measure your KPIs.

7. Avoid getting distracted by data discoveries unrelated to the task in hand.

8. Do NOT use the data to support a preconceived idea.

9. Be assured it's cheaper to fail on paper, which data enables you to do via modelling.

10. If you are holding Consumer data - protect it!

It's not just the big corporates under attack for example the recent Graff hack where a cyber gang stole a list of 11,000 high worth client details and posted some online with the threat of revealing more unless they paid a ransom. In preparation for the CIBJO panel, I contacted 3 local cyber security companies and asked for a ballpark quote for protecting a data base of 10,000 clients – the process seemed to be an initial audit /

vulnerability check at a cost between £500 and £1,000, and an average £100 a month servicing cost subject to your system / requirements. The cost is not prohibitive, though perhaps the question you should be asking yourself is, what's the cost to the business of not securing your clients data?

11. Benchmark your performance data with other businesses in your sector, as they say apples with apples. How else will you know if you are going a good job or a not so good job?

12. And finally check your data regularly looking for trends, and patterns, and be prepared to react accordingly.

I once worked for a very energetic MD who taught me the two fingered salute - by running two fingers down columns of data reporting year on year performance and budget performance looking for double deficits. Once any double deficits had been identified, I'd be threatened with his two-fingered salute, if I hadn't eradicated them within 3 months.

As in most things, the important thing about getting started is, just getting started. But be mindful other SMEs, potentially those competing with you, are already using data to reduce their risks, gain competitive market advantage, drive their growth, and improve their bottom line.

So, what's stopping you doing the same thing?

-68-
Does your company have a growth culture?

2018

Here are the three essentials of a growth culture, a few key questions to challenge your thinking and a handful of helpful tips to get your growth started.

Process
Today many companies are growing profits faster than sales, thanks in no small part to automation and cost cutting, which isn't sustainable and sometime sooner or later they are going to need a sales growth strategy – as there'll be nothing left to cut.

There are many businesses with a wonderful heritage and a strong legacy that are no longer growing and are happy just to see that back of last year and the start of a new year to face the same old same old.

- What type of growth do you want to achieve?
- How are you going to measure it?
- How ambitious are your growth goals?
- Who do you bench mark your performance against?

The plan doesn't have to be complicated and it doesn't need to be pages and pages, but you do need a plan that covers the 5 basics of: the business you are in, the business you want to be in, the route to get there, the required resources and a defined understanding of how you will recognise, when you've got there.

After all, if you fail to prepare, then prepare to fail.

You will need to identify what you are going to do differently, that will make the difference to your previous performance – sense check it, resource it, START it, tweak it, and deliver it. Otherwise accept that, what you've always done you'll always get (if you're lucky).

People
Customers today want to share (social media) they want personalisation not just in the product but in the purchase experience (and beyond). You need to walk in your customers shoes to really understand how they feel when they walk in store, go online, phone you, email you, seek information, make a purchase, return a product.

Customers are an asset that you build up over time, think of it literally as a relationship whether that's new, current, or lapsed – as we all know we get out what we put in. Relationships evolve and require different attention at different times, some demand more time and effort, some can be casual and relaxed, others stressed and uncomfortable; and it's no different to your customer relationships (including your internal customers). For each there are different levels of engagement.

>How often do you "speak" to your customers?
>How often do you see/engage with the same customers?
>What keeps your customers coming back?
>What insights are you gathering from them?

How often do we hear it's a people business, the people are the real asset of this business, without the people we wouldn't have a business – great sentiments or hollow platitudes or a people first culture... you decide.

Investment of time and money in your people so they can either be promoted to take on greater responsibility or equipped with the skills and capabilities to safeguard the future of your business is critical to any growth culture.

> When did you last attract top talent?
> Do your people understand their roles, responsibilities, and performance expectations?
> Do you have a blame culture, or do you learn from failure?
> Are you building the right capabilities for the future?

Product

> Cliché Warning:
> *'If new product is the life blood of any business,*
> *why do so many companies need a blood transfusion?'*

Probably because what they bring to market isn't unique, doesn't satisfy a recognised need or simply isn't good enough to attract new customers. Or they have a great product (but aren't they all, otherwise why launch them) which hasn't been marketed properly, so why should it sell.

> Great products or Great marketing – which one matters most?
> How centric is marketing in your business?

Apple is almost as famous for its launch marketing as it is for its product innovation. Pandora's marketing transformed a common bead into a globally recognised jewellery brand. P&G's product and marketing teams transformed a failing Oil of Olay into a $2B+ Olay brand.

Growth companies are successful because they are customer centric and driven by ambitious goals.

-69-
We don't know what we don't know

2021

I'd just finished delivering a short podium session at an exhibition in Earl's Court, London when I was approached by a former colleague. We exchanged a few pleasantries and agreed to meet up very soon for a proper catch-up, and they were off, their parting words ringing in my ears "we don't know what we don't know".

It was an odd thing to say in the context (or had I missed something) and I often wondered what they had meant by it. In later years as a management consultant, I have grasped more of its value within in the context of "knowing what we know". For example, if I don't believe I'm able to add value to a client business or their people, I pass on the details of someone who could do a better *'job'* than I could, rather than attempt to *'wing-it'*.

Many proport that the origins of this saying are in the Donald Rumsfeld, (US secretary of defence) 2002 interview on WMD - weapons of mass destruction.

> *"As we know, there are known knowns; there are things we know we know. We also know there are known unknowns; that is to say we know there are some things we do not know. But there are also unknown unknowns - the ones we don't know we don't know".*

Others believe it goes back to the clearer thinking of Socrates the Greek philosopher almost two and a half thousand years earlier, who sought to understand wisdom, in the context of awareness and knowledge and the desire to remain curious and open. As illustrated by the Sklar Wilton matrix below.

	Knowledge yes	Knowledge no
Awareness yes	Things you know that you know	Things you know that you don't know
Awareness no	Things you don't know that you know	Things that you don't know that you don't know

Each quartile positions a choice and a response, even if it's a passive response to ignore it and do nothing. All active responses require, as Socrates said: self-awareness, curiosity, openness to receive and change. Many business leaders, busy doing the doing, fail to see there's even a choice to be made.

Let's take a quick look at each quartile:

Things you know that you know *(Awareness Yes Knowledge Yes)*
Put simply doing what you do day in day out like commuting to work, serving customers, meeting clients, flying planes, teaching children, running businesses.

Things that you don't know that you know *(Awareness No Knowledge Yes)* **Best** illustrated by the conversations and interactions we have with others - think back to the 2020 zoom quizzes and the oft uttered words "I don't know where that came from". Or being able to follow a conversation littered with acronyms NAJ, IoD, C2S, WBS, JBN, MCFC are you still following?

Or in listening to a client, you are able to understand, relate and contribute to the conversation, even though you have never actually worked in their sector.

Things that you know you don't know *(Awareness Yes Knowledge No)*
I know how to drive my car, how to refuel, how to check the tyre pressure, how to work the hands-free phone etc but when it comes to servicing or strange engine noises, I know my limitations and I go to my local garage because they know what I don't know.
In business a situation it usually results in the leader deciding to either learn how to do it themselves (assuming they have the luxury of time) or delegating to a colleague or hiring a consultant.

Things you don't know you don't know *(Awareness No Knowledge No)*.
I recently received a quote to have a collapsed drain grill replaced and received two quotes, one was a fixed price, the other was open-ended; because they didn't know what else they might find wrong once they started the work. The contactor knew what they didn't know, and the customer (me) had no awareness or knowledge of what might exist under the collapsed drain cover.

In general life, these are our blind spots - the things we are not aware of, they are our unknowns. Awareness of your unknowns makes you also aware that an unknown for you is likely known by someone else – as a business leader such awareness encourages you to avoid recruiting in your own likeness, to increase the diversity of the team and to hire the external expert as and when required. Though as a white, middle-aged, middle class, male, I'm probably not the best candidate to assist on improving boardroom diversity and inclusion, but I do know someone who knows!

-70-
Do YOU run your business, or does IT run you?

2017

Aside from the few occasions that can best be described as: it's got to be done now, the I'll be home late tonight call or the Saturday morning in the office just to catch up - are you the one who runs the business, manages its people, and takes the decisions or are you run by it?
Do you spend more time reacting to situations than you do on proactive activities? Are you too busy even now, to read let alone consider the following, that could help you reduce anxiety levels, release more time and enable you to run a more effective business for all involved.

How many of these attitudes and behaviours do you need to manage in yourself or your people?

Time Thieves - the *"have you got a minute"*, the *"I just need to tell you that zzzzzzzzzz"*, the *"I'm too busy to do anything else"* people. They need help managing themselves or they need managing out.

Delegation Dilemmas - of course it's probably too important to delegate after all *"if a job's worth doing, it's worth doing well"* but it'll never happen unless you try, try, and try again until you get it right - you may even be surprised that your staff do a better job than you ever did.

Trust Trials - if it really is a problem to let go, start with the small things, not necessarily the company credit card or the keys to the factory and as your trust grows allow the amount of responsibility you share to grow - it'll work wonders for you and those around you.

Responsibility Rewards - acknowledge, thank, and where appropriate praise - which is often reward enough especially if it doesn't happen very often. But also, be generous when you can - a late start, an early finish, or a meal out for those having to stay away on weekend business can go a long way to show your appreciation and build an employee's sense of worth.

Holiday Hots - the days of self-imposed stress and anxiety leading up to a holiday and immediately following a holiday, as you try to clear your in-tray before of everything that should have been done sooner or could realistically wait till you get back. The lost few days towards the end of the holiday as you anticipate what you'll face when you get back to your desk, and the oft heard *"I need another holiday"* within the first few days of your return – all of which could be avoided if you managed yourself better.

Reasons Reasons Reasons - time after time, why something was not done, or targets not achieved; you may appear to be listening, but you switched off long ago. The solution is not simple and it's not quick, but it works, remove the obstacles, and provide everything required to achieve what needs to be done or remove the people, because *"if you can't change the people change the people"*.

Present with a Purpose - *"sorry I can't talk now I'm going into a meeting"* or "I'm afraid he is in a meeting can I take a message". Learn to say no to meeting invitations, and to only invite those who need to be present in your meetings, you or your staff don't have time to warm seats and the meeting will be shorter and more effective without passengers. In time the habit will spread, and the released meeting hours will make a positive impact on the life and soul of the business.

By changing the way, you, or your staff work, you can take back control of your business and be much happier in the process.

-71-
Cultural cows and cakes could close you!

2022

Company Owners and Leaders, I speak with are expressing increased concern, worry and in some cases anxiety about the threat of pests to their businesses and I'm not talking about cockroaches, rodents, or rogues but the PESTS, the political, economic, social, and technology challenges to their business.

You know the BIG things that even governments struggle to respond to let alone control – the threats of cyber-attacks, supply chain inflation, mental health issues, technology advances, climate change, new viruses, environmental crisis, cost of living hikes, wage demands, Brexit, UK devolution, US civil unrest and war in Europe.

BUT with every challenge comes opportunity… yet to realise opportunity you must first challenge your sacred cows and your cake making.

A sacred cow is a closely held belief that is beyond question, immune from criticism, and effectively untouchable!

I recall first hearing (and understanding) the phrase when a marketing agency pitching for our business asked, *"are there any sacred cows in the business, areas where we can't go, people products or processes we must not touch?"*

Cakes are a more current (GBBO) translation of Henry Ford's *"If you always do what you've always done, you'll always get what you've always got"*, in that *"You can't use the same ingredients and expect to bake a different cake."*

I was once a BUM before being promoted to a Business Unit Director... becoming responsible for the unit's profit generation, which was being held back by a number of personally held sacred cows.

One particular growth opportunity required changing the habits (work and personal) of a lifetime.

The marketing team saw an opportunity for profit growth by offering next day delivery on all orders placed by 3pm, yet to achieve this we had to increase/plan our stock better, manage our order loading, ensure the process flow was sufficiently resourced to handle any spikes and take our staff with us, all of which required a business unit team effort to deliver.

It involved lots of internal and external negotiations, for example having royal mail and other carriers move their collection times back to suit us, and changing staff start and finish times. Not as easy as you think if you've inherited a post room team working factory hours because the post room had always reported into the factory and that's how it had always been 7.30am starts and 3.30pm finish, with a lunch time finish on a Friday... not great if you want afternoon orders delivered next day!

So, we had to consider mixing up the ingredients to get the cake we wanted... a few agreed to the new hours but not all, so we'd move staff from other areas in the business unit from 3.30pm onwards into the post room. We replaced leavers with new starters on new hours, but the sweetest moment was when John (post room man and boy) agreed some 12 months after the changes to change his hours and the reason ... *"I can see that the changes were right for the business"* in that they offered greater job security and job satisfaction.

The business quickly went on to achieve market leadership with a 98.5% on time delivery, in full, on all orders placed by 4pm, generated more sales, employed more people, and before it became a sacred cow.

I dialled back a percentage point or two on the delivery, saved hundreds of thousands on stock holding, boosted profits, and still retained our market leadership positioning.

What are your sacred cows?
- Managers who are allowed to treat staff badly.
- Pet projects led by the Boss.
- Unprofitable products that used to be best sellers.
- Best sellers that are now unprofitable.
- Out of date services.
- Antiquated technology (small t) loved by the staff disliked by the customer.
- Services that no longer resonate with the latest generation of customers.
- Hours of work.
- Holiday policy.
- Place of work.

Covid put Cows and Cakes on the senior managements to-do list, and many took decisions for the survival and prosperity of the business that would have been considered strictly out of bounds a year or so before; others sat it out thanks in no small part to the government support, which won't be so generous with the next PEST.

Why do we continue to do stuff that we have always done, stuff that's been handed down through the generations, stuff that is not as effective as it used to be?

When did you last seriously question or challenge your cows and cakes in terms of what they bring to your post covid business, let alone what they bring to your business in the current or threatened political, economic, social, technology challenges?

Challenge doesn't have to be complicated, but it can be difficult - that's why it called a challenge.

10 Helpful pointers to get you started:

1. Start the conversation.
2. Restate your values why purpose.
3. Be sensitive.
4. All ideas count.
5. Provide a process framework.
6. Start on one of your cows that no one expects you to offer up.
7. Be specific not fluffy.
8. Acknowledge concerns like job security.
9. Define what *"good"* looks like.
10. Share the financials.

One of the biggest blockers for Owners, Leaders, and Employees, when it comes to cows and cakes is FEAR … but be encouraged others have been there, been through it and survived to share their experiences.

"The only man who makes no mistakes is the man who never does anything." Theodore Roosevelt – US President

"The difficulty lies not in new ideas but in escaping from the old ones, which ramify, for those brought up as most as has been, into every corner of our minds." John Maynard Keynes - Economist

"We need to have the confidence that the way we are working is the best way to work - if not, we need to change the way we work."
Michael Donaldson - The Value Innovator

-72-
Menopause needs men to implement the Menostart

2022

Women make up 56% of the UK workforce and 100% of women experience the menopause. That's potentially over half of an organisation's workforce suffering from the physical, mental, and emotional symptoms of hot flushes, night terrors, lack of sleep, confidence, and self-worth. Along with increased forgetfulness, irritation, frustration, anxiety, and stress. Which not only affects them but affects their immediate relationships with partners, families, and work colleagues.

Yet only 10% of organisations are doing anything about menopause in their businesses.

WARNING 2022 WARNING
If you want to retain your talent, be more profitable and an employee of choice, you will have to address the issue of menopause in the workforce, as ignorance is no longer an acceptable excuse.

At this point you've either got the point or
you're thinking what's the point.

Then here's some context for the point, I've worked and lived with those going through the menopause and I assure you it's not that easy for men either, but the catalyst for this blog came from attending a recent session organised by Circle2Success on the impact of the menopause by Miss Menopause Sharon MacArthur.

Here's another interesting fact that torpedoed my misperception of *"going through the menopause"* and I quote *"women spend a third of their lives in menopause."*

Clearly most men leading businesses need to recognise the related issues of the menopause, understand them, accept them, and then manage them, for the benefit of their employee's wellbeing and business performance.

In business I can recall assuming women flushing when presenting was simply down to nerves and that barked instructions or snappy emails down to not being able to handle the pressure of the job.

I remember in one of my early roles a senior female colleague shouting at me *"pull over, pull over"* (I was driving on the M62 to company meeting) then in no uncertain terms being told to *"get out of the car! I'll drive or we'll never get there!"* I was doing 70mph at the time and hadn't realised a Mark 5 Ford Cortina could hit the speeds we hit. Yet we did arrive on time, and the only damage done was to our fledgling relationship, which never really took off after that incident.

I remember offering a woman a promotion at work, an offer that generated tears unfortunately they weren't tears of happiness and a few days later she declined the offer due to "personal circumstances." At the time I put it down to a lack of ambition and commitment to the business.

A few years later she felt able to share the real reasons with me, as well as telling me that at the time she felt my response to her tears was cold (I thought I was being professional) and formal (I thought I was trying to react to her as I would a male colleague). Hey Ho, we live and learn.

At home I've been learning not to complaint about another broken night's sleep or to offer solutions or pep talks when an extended lie in or silent hug or a cup of tea would be more appreciated!

So, what can we men do to start to address something that affects over half the working population (at some time or other) in our organisations, to enable them to work through it to the benefit of both parties?

Here are my five suggestions to help get the menostart started:

1. Remove the do not go there label currently on the issue.

2. Context it with what you are doing to support other issues that affect smaller percentages of your employees.

3. Consider how your current position sits with your organisations Equality Policy.

4. Engage the Women in your organisation (Ask, Listen & Learn) and normalise the conversation.

5. Involve the experts just as you would on any other employee issue - in this case I'd recommend contacting Miss Menopause - you'll find her on LinkedIn or at https://www.missmenopause.co.uk/

And for any women still reading please share this with the men you know leading organisations – you know we can be slow on the uptake, especially if we've stuck a don't go there, label on it!

-73-
A GOAL without a plan is just a WISH

2020

After 30 years in what is generically referred to as "corporate life" where we even planned the plan, the shock of working with smaller businesses that do not produce a plan, let alone written goals was (for me) an anathema – I just didn't get it!

The vast majority of SMEs I speak to say that they want to grow their business, that GROWTH is their number ONE GOAL, yet the majority of them don't have a written plan on how they are going to achieve their most important business goal. Countless UK surveys report that SMEs do not write business plans or goals (Barclays Bank 2017 survey 23%, Close Brothers Asset Finance 2018 survey 29% and my own 2019 survey 46%).

The reasons given for not writing a plan of any sort, are numerous: they don't see the point or benefit for one, they have done alright without one, it's in their head, they are too busy in the business to find the time to write one let alone implement one, they have enough paperwork to do. They don't need to justify their performance or seek sign-off from anyone else, as it's their business and ultimately the buck stops with them.

Their overriding sentiment being one of "there's never been enough time in the day to really review, what's the best way forward for the business, we're simply too busy doing the doing to find out" – which I get but as I said it's an anathema to me.

Over the years I've had to write lots of plans and goals, particularly if I wanted to spend the company's money. I had to show how it would be spent, what the goals were and what the return would be – all very sensible. Some were approved, some required a tweak, and some never got the support to go any further. I remember writing one particularly brilliant plan, it was over 50 pages long, with appendices, graphs and tables; had a concise executive summary, contents table, it covered every angle, anticipated every possible question and took the readers through a very persuasive case for support ... it was a textbook business plan.

I can still recall the words of our US CEO

> *"Michael it's a great plan but we can get a better return putting our money in a bank account - Thanks for your time".*

Are you a planner or a dreamer?

Are you a guesser, a chaser, do you fly by the seat of your pants, love solving problems, addressing the issue of the day, are you the best fire fighter in the business and possible its only arsonist or do you simply cross your fingers and wish upon a star when it comes to the future of your business?

Why plan?

A plan forces you to prioritise what you do and don't do in terms of what will help achieve the plan, it stops you being distracted, it challenges any tendency you may have to do stuff (you particularly enjoy) that doesn't progress the plan and it ensures the most important tasks are done. It enables you to track the progress of your business, make any adjustments and celebrate success – because you now know what it looks like. In short, it gives you daily focus the moment you start work, which increases your motivation, confidence, and self-esteem.

It also has enormous associated benefits in that it reduces worry and anxiety; and gives you time to live outside work without constantly thinking about work. I'd say these were compelling reasons for taking your business seriously and finding the time to plan the plan.

I once received a call from an MD who said, *"I know I need help; I just don't know where to start".*

Three points to remember at this point ...

> It doesn't have to be complicated.
> It doesn't have to be 50 pages long.
> It does have to be right for the moment your business is in.

Remember the CEO above – their real issue at that moment was the length of time their plan would have taken to deliver the return, they wanted more, faster.

How to write your first plan?

Here's an outline that I recommend for people thinking about planning and writing down business goals for the first time, that can be achieved on 2 sides of paper, in 3 steps, and 4 questions.

I call it the ONE PAGE PLAN – there are hundreds of variants available online, but I think this is a good starting point for those who have never really written a plan before, and it only takes 20 -30 minutes to complete.

One Goal - Three Objectives - Five Actions

What is the one goal you want to achieve in your business?

What do you have to change in your business to achieve that goal?

What 3 objectives do you need to set and achieve to bring about the required change?

What 5 actions do you need to do to achieve each of the 3 objectives?

-74-
WeWork not as we use too - Culture Challenge
2019

The world of work has changed, and it hasn't all been for the good – or is it just another generational thing. I can remember my father bemoaning the end of national service and today I often hear the gripe about Gen Z & Millennial sense of entitlement. Whether it's out with the old and in with the new – the challenge our business leaders face is in knowing when to stop, drop, embrace, and evolve!

We no longer make "things" ...
Services are the sector that account for the largest part of the economy – in 2017, they accounted for 79% of economic output, the production sector for 14%, construction for 6% and agriculture for 1% (UK Parliament Papers)

We no longer work in the "traditional" office ...
Partitions were ripped out long ago, desks are increasing being replaced with tables, private meeting rooms are glass sided fish tanks and chairs no longer have four legs.

We no longer work in organisations with 10's of 000's of employees...
There were 5.7 million SMEs in the UK in 2018, which was over 99% of all businesses. (UK Parliament Papers)

We no longer provide young people with the right skills...
Most employer surveys indicate a demand for technical and job-specific skills while also demanding a wide array of general employability skills, such as communication, teamwork, and

commercial awareness, with entrepreneurial and data analysis skills increasingly being added to that to list... with one in three graduates being "mismatched" to the jobs they find after leaving university. (Universities UK)

We no longer stay with the same company for life...
In the UK we typically have 6 different jobs in 6 different companies across our working life. (The Association of Accounting Technicians Poll 2015)

We no longer allow our managers to manage...
Many are in roles to oversee the work of their people, enforce policy, communicate decisions, report results, escalate issues, and generally administer stuff. They are not being released from their non-value adding activities and empowered to make a difference, on the spot.

I recently made a best practice visit to a blue-chip manufacturing business currently trialling 5G, but the one thing that provoked more conversation was how they faced the challenges to their culture from new technology and new recruits. On a micro level the cultural challenges within organisations today irrespective of their size, shape, or sector, seem to be emotionally polarised and at times paralysed by correctness - depending on your age, gender, career path and opinion!

Here are some examples of cultural challenges gleaned from my post visit conversations with SMEs:

New starters expecting and requesting holiday parity with long servers.

Emails written as texts e.g., do NOT contact Mark Smith again.

Messaging a partner on Facebook whilst participating in 3 separate customer chat room conversations.

A staff member asserting their right to further increased study time to retake a failed exam.

The widespread policy that staff in open plan offices can listen to music on their headphones and in some cases the same practice applies on the shop floor - where one person was found watching a film.

A home worker running software that made mouse movements and keystrokes on their laptop - whilst they caught up on their sleep.

Freedom to update social media at work, at any time.

The provision of sofas, ping-pong tables, quiet spaces, and unlimited smoothies for when staff felt the need to step away.

A choice of how and where staff want to work; at a coffee table, on the sofa or at an adjustable height desk with the option of a hokki chair.

Conversations framed and designed to elicit desired responses for the device concealed in the pocket.

It's not surprising culture provokes so much conversation!

The employees of the best practice company I visited invested time, energy, and emotion, from the shop floor up - to creating their own culture. In the boardroom they recognised that it's better to understand, rather than dismiss the push backs on the existing culture AND started their debate with Why Not?

Company culture drives the *"who we are, the how we do things here"* - a weak culture costs you money in performance.

Where a weak culture exists growth plans and acquisitions struggle to deliver the intended results due to staff chaos, confusion, and frustration – with a strong culture there's no such fog and its widely adopted and enhanced during the integration / initiation process.

Lost millions that could have been avoided with a strong culture.

Employee happiness had *"a substantial positive correlation with customer loyalty"* (aka better business) states a Gallup Poll of 1.9m employees across 230 separate organisations in 73 countries.

So back to the challenge raised at the top of the chapter, knowing when to stop, drop, embrace, and evolve!

Here are my 5 tips - forged in the experience of success and failure:

1. Know your culture.

2. Live your culture.

3. Understand the demands on your culture.

4. Identify the external risks to your culture.

5. Evolve your culture - but only if it adds value to your stakeholders, your people, your customers.

-75-
Are you in control of your cyber creep?

2016

Has your personal life succumbed to the cyber habits of the office? Cyber creep is killing conversations and undermining relationships at work and at home - a survey by Good Technology reported that 69% of staff check their emails before they go to bed!

Are you living a cyber life - one that is spent on the internet?

A One Poll survey suggests we spend 9 hours a day in the UK looking at a screen and check our mobile phones 200 times a day – assuming the average person is awake for 18 hours a day then we spend half our life looking at a screen and check our phone every 5 minutes.

McKinsey Global Institute said that office staff spends over 25% of their time during the working day writing and responding to emails and that was 3 years ago!

The Global Web Index says in the UK we are active on an average of 4 social networks each (for example LinkedIn, Facebook, You Tube and Twitter) and spend an average 1 hour 50 minutes each day managing them! No wonder more of us are wearing glasses *"Just under 60 per cent of Britons now wear prescription glasses or contact lenses on a regular basis"* (research analysts Taylor Nelson Sofres).

The pressure on our children to live a cyber life means they are not only missing out on real world experiences but are at risk of being ill equipped for what life throws at them as they grow up.

Speaking with a business owner in Educational Toys I was shown The Key, State of Education survey 2016. The research suggests alarming numbers of four and five-year-olds could be behind in a range of ways, including delayed speech and social skills. Some of the 1,100 respondents blamed mobile technology's intrusion on family life and one primary school head teacher said, *"Four-year-olds know how to swipe a phone but haven't a clue about conversations."*

Living a cyber life is not just a Western issue, the Chinese use the term *"Indoorsy"* to describe people who to choose to stay at home, depending on cyber communication with the outside world. Activities that traditionally required the individual to leave the home can now be fulfilled without going out... they can speak to family and friends, play team games online, make new friends, find life partners, study for a new career, shop and download entertainment.

I recently found myself questioning the extent to which cyber creep had encroached on my life – sitting down for a 'holiday' lunch with 3 friends we all instinctively placed our mobiles on the table. Enjoying pre-dinner drinks with clients the vibration in my pocket alerted me to a text (one I was expecting from my daughter) as the conversation continued, I took a quick glance and responded with a couple of finger taps before switching it off and slipping it back in my pocket. The affront to my conscience was that a year earlier I would have explained I was expecting a text and asked if anyone minded if I responded before switching the phone off.

In the not-too-distant future successful businesses will require two skill sets, human skills, and cyber skills, yet I have a genuine concern that the drive for the latter will be at the expense of the former, that communication will be cyber driven and not face to face. The same One Poll survey encouragingly reports that 50% of those surveyed *"felt technology has made us worse at communicating with each other".*

Businesses need to invest in their people as well as their processes if they are to add value and differentiate themselves in today's cyber world.

-76-
Five step process to successful Range Management
2018

In the summer of 2017 Burberry made the headlines for having destroyed £28m of (unsold) stock to guard against counterfeits - a practice understood to be common across the retail industry. According to the Times, more than £90m of Burberry products have been destroyed over the past five years. A company spokesman said: *"Burberry has careful processes in place to minimise the amount of excess stock we produce."*

What a gift that headline that was, as I put my finishing touches to a client session on how to generate more sales from range management.

I've ranged product from bars of soap to bars of gold, coffee makers to carpet and it isn't or shouldn't be complicated; but it's often seen as a dull, number crunching, thankless task, especially when trying to recruit in today's digital obsessed world, where the very basics of range management appear no longer relevant let alone appealing – it's more than just posting, it's about profitable sales too!

In prepping for the session, I came across these key responsibilities I'd written a decade or so earlier for a Product Manager:

1. To develop and manage a designated product range so that the offer remains comprehensive, competitive, and profitable.

2. To ensure each product category is maximising its contribution to the business through the Product Life Cycle.

3. To ensure that the service propositions are effectively in place to meet customer expectations and company financial targets.

Which is all very well for the larger businesses that can afford to employ teams of marketers and product managers to sit alongside their data analysts - something which is often beyond the resources (or desire) of the SME. But that's no excuse for SMEs because effective range management is not rocket science, but YOU do have to find the time to do or lead it within your business until it's embedded in the process culture.

To help get you thinking about range management, here's my 5-step process that's served me well across a variety of sectors.

Step One: Understand & Define

What business are you in?

What business do your customers think you are in?
This is easier to answer than you think, just look at the specific number of items you sell, for example a watch retailer who only sells 1 watch a week and 1,000 watch batteries a week is clearly perceived by their customers as the place to go for watch batteries not watches. If you don't know what specific business you are in, how will your customers know – this is an important first step, as it add customer centricity to your process.

How does your range enhance your brand?

What does your range offer your customers?

Step Two: Review & Decide

Know your target customer - the clearer you are the more likely you are to engage them.
Make your data visual & bring it to life, physically spread it out in front of you. I used a "runners and riders" board for carpet, an idea suggested to me by a multiple retail buyer with a passion for horse racing. On the wall of my office were my top 25 best sellers running left to right, with the best-selling colours running top to bottom – over 500 swatches, which were repositioned monthly with the latest sales data. It's true a picture is worth a thousand words.

Fill your data gaps, it exists somewhere in your business; so just collect it and don't accept vague answers from yourself or your people.

If this sounds all too much in terms of what you are doing now then keep it simple, get your range out in front of you and identify product duplication, gaps and similarities, that alone would be worth doing yourself, as you'll learn so much about the shortcomings in your range.

Step Three: Seek & Find

For some of the businesses I worked in, this step would have covered several product options within the range such as: make, buy, hybrid, generic or exclusive.

Yet the process steps within step three, were common and put simply as:
Write a shopping / new product development list.
Write a specification.
Set your budget.
Know your sell price.
Be clear on the margin.
Remember the range fit.

Hold the customer proposition.

Today finding product couldn't be easier – just asked Google.

The challenge is spending your money with reputable suppliers, who not only deliver a product on time, in full, fit for purpose and on the price; but meet product & business compliance requirements as a given.
They show a genuine interest in being part of your business growth, provide a stream of new ideas and are a pleasure to deal with – as I said it's a challenge, but these suppliers once found should be encouraged to become "part of the family" or in consultancy speak - strategic partners.

Step Four: Present & Sell

The first step in true Gallagher brother nuance - What's the story?

If this is not a unique product, how are your competitors selling similar products?

Do you want to imitate or differentiate?

What experience are you offering?

Ensure every proposed activity builds & reinforces the perception of the business you want to be in. Agree the approach and then train, train, train your people. The key is to get your people as excited about it, as you were when you sourced / made it.

Step Five: Review & Act

Thinking back to the key responsibilities above, review your range performance by answering the following half dozen questions at least once a year.

Q: comprehensive? competitive? profitable? maximising its contribution?

Q: meeting customer expectations? delivering company financial targets?

To ACT WISELY on what you now know, is probably the hardest aspect of range management as it demands a considered head decision not a passionate heart decision - for the profit is in the detail of your Range Management.

-77-

Whether it's BIG DATA or small data, if you don't use it - it's just data!

2014

According to CMS Wire, marketeers who put data at the centre of their marketing decisions can increase their ROI by 15-20%.

In our daily lives we are making hundreds and potentially thousands of decisions every day, some are complicated, some carry greater risk, some are harder to implement and some need more reliable data.

We all process data to some degree or other, but ever noticed how the successful companies use it more than others in their decision-making process?

When "Antennagate" was raging round the launch of the iPhone 4, Steve Jobs was on holiday, and rather than react to the emotion and suggestion, he stayed on the beach with the family - until the data confirmed the existence and size of the problem. When he then returned to his office and said, *"OK here's the data what do we do?"*

Ever wonder why Banks are always advertising new and improved services?

Because the data shows that 3% of all Banking customers change their bank every year, for better services and ease of use.

Data can guide decisions on where to spend your marketing budget - Domino's Pizza took the decision to the increase the budget for digital marketing from 38% to 51% in 2014 based on the data that showed a shift to online and mobile order placement.

Looking to differentiate themselves in the Betting market Ladbrokes rolled out a re-launch to all 2,300+ stores based on the test market results from just 10 stores - so convincing was the data.

During my time at Breville, data decisions (along with a creative TV ad) increased our market share by 10.6% in the critical Christmas period.

So, when using data in your decision-making process, try to remember these 5 principles.

1. Rubbish in means Rubbish out.

2. Know what you want from the data.

3. Know how you want to manipulate the data.

4. Don't use the data to support a preconceived idea.

5. And it's cheaper to fail on paper.

-78-
Key Performance Indicators – love them or loathe them, here are 10 tips to help you use them rather than abuse them.

2014

1. Do remember they are ONLY Indicators.

2. Don't have too many - they can distract from the real issues.

3. Do use selectively on the things that matter.

4. Don't ignore the input of those who work in the area when defining the KPI for the area.

5. Do spend time on the creation of specific rate and score questions for engagement areas.

6. Don't assume one size will fit across all functions.

7. Do monitor, discuss, and share regularly.

8. Don't assume high customer satisfaction ratings will guarantee customer loyalty.

9. Do review their continued relevance to the business.

10. Don't collect data for data sake.

-79-
Have you reviewed your Annual Plan yet as it could already be out of date?

2014

The new year may only be 3 weeks old, but your plan could already be out of date. These 5 quick checks highlight the areas most likely to have changed since the plan was written and will save you not only time and money but emotion and reputation.

1. Probably written four months ago with figures just as old, now is the time to update your Plan forecast figures with actual previous year figures - any surprises?

2. Review actual customer performance and trading status - has anything changed?

3. Consider your competition - did any launch new products or services that surprised you and could impact your Plan?

4. What are the rumours circulating about your suppliers, how did they trade in the last quarter - are there potential issues that could disrupt your supply chain?

5. New Year and lots of resolutions about finding a new job. Have any of your key staff indicated they are about to leave or even resigned - if so, what impact will that have on the Plan, and what's the status of your succession plan?

Review completed it is now time to get your teams together to re/present this year's Annual Plan in the context of last year's performance and your general strategy.

-80-
Marketing - only as good as your brief!

2022

If you can't explain what you want, the listener won't understand what you want, you'll both be disappointed, and the only guaranteed output is the cost.

How good are your staff at briefing colleagues or external agencies, in precisely what your expectations are?

In an organisation, questions were being asked by the board about the actual value generated by the marketing budget, and I was invited to understand and address the issues behind the negative perceptions, that they were being failed by their agency and that a change was long overdue.

And it's always easier to blame an external "partner" than an internal "partner," because they resist answering back for fear of losing the business, and it's often seen by the client as a disposable or temporary relationship – which is not good for any relationship in business or life in general.

What became apparent following a number of round table conversations with the agency, and the organisation's head of marketing, was that the contracted 100 hours a month were being wasted!

In the preceding four months, actual hours (not fully billed because the agency didn't want to jeopardise their relationship), against the contracted 100 monthly hours, were 139 hours, 293 hours, 112 hours, and 132 hours. UNBELIEVABLE - until you realise it had taken 4 hours to sign-off an email, 8 hours to sign off a compliments slip, 54 hours to sign off a postcard and 100 hours to sign off a certificate.

> *"If you can't explain what you want,*
> *the listener won't understand what you want,*
> *you'll both be disappointed, and the only guaranteed output is the cost."*

We turned this situation round very quickly with two simple actions:

We secured a template for a Creative Brief from the agency, which covered everything they would need to know, to deliver the job to the client's expectations.

We introduced a "No Brief No work" rule and applied it to all internal requests for marketing, the marketing team, and the agency.

The following four months hours came in at 38 hours, 22 hours, 6 hours, and 284 hours.

Gradually, held perceptions became more positive (or negative ones were not vocalised as often), individual relationships between the agency and the organisation improved, as both parties fully understood what was expected of each other, and importantly the board were happier, as the marketing costs came down as the hours purchased fell.

Here's the 12 question Creative Brief template supplied all those years ago, but still as valuable today as it was then.

1. What is required?

2. What size and format is it required to take?

3. Where and to whom are we supplying the finished work or items?

4. What exactly is the brief?

5. Who are we talking to?

6. What is the single most important thing we want to communicate?

7. What are the reasons to believe?

8. What tone and manner should we adopt?

9. Any mandatories we should consider?

10. Deliverables?

11. Anything else?

12. What are the deadlines and timeframes?

If your agency is not asking these questions - it's time to change your agency.

If your team are not answering these questions - it's time to ask questions of your team.

-81-
How to be found in a crowded market

2021

It will help if you think in terms of the 3E's.

Exposure, Expenditure, and Experience.

In 2013 we were exposed to over 7,000 brand messages every day, in 2020 the figure is estimated to be closer to 10,000 a day, which is not all that surprising given the explosion of digital marketing in the last decade and a record UK adverting spend of £26Billion last year - thus within seconds of landing on any digital page we are bombarded with irritating ads!

How do you survive and prosper if you are one of the UK's 560 gin distilleries, 9,435 jewellers, 60,000 management consultants or 250,000 marketing agencies; without spending a million let alone a billion on advertising?

Consider Experience in terms what you offer and deliver, and what your customers receive and value, and focus on your core expertise - it does not have to be complicated; it could be as simple as:

People (leadership and mentoring)
Product (profitability and positioning)
Process (planning and strategy)

Surely, it's not all about Emojis and Stars?

What used to be the domain of restaurants and hotels is now on everything from Amazon deliveries to Gas BBQ's, Face Creams, Hedge Trimmers, and the length of time spent in a queue … and we do read them, and they do influence our purchase decisions.

As a *"me-only-company"* with a limited marketing budget, it was not surprising that after my first 5 years in business only 4% of my assignments could be classified as new business from a new contact, which was worrying until put in the context of where the majority of my assignments came from – people who knew me or were told about me! (29% from former colleagues and 42% from referrals).

> *"When hiring a management consulting firm, clients do not know what they are getting in advance, because they are looking for knowledge that they themselves lack. They cannot measure the results, either because outside factors, such as the quality of execution, influence the outcome of the consultant recommendations – so they rely on reputation."*
> Clayton Christensen Harvard Business School

In other words what the customer says about you - Referrals help cut through the noise and confusion of a crowded market, so don't forget to ask for them.

-82-
How to attract and retain NEW customers
2021

If you want new customers and you want to retain them, make their experience easy and enjoyable – it's not complicated. B2B is more about making the life of a buyer easier, and B2C is more about making the purchase pleasurable.

Here are ten lessons for getting it right, set in the context of the High Street and Hotels, something we can all relate too.

I've missed both but my recent experiences in more cases than not have been anything but easy, and enjoyable. In fact, I thought I was getting old and grumpy before my time, so I co-opted 6 independent retail owners and asked them to share their thoughts and experiences following a day on the high street mystery shopping, which turned out to be enlightening and encouraging but not for the reasons you might think!

3years ago I purchased a pair of walking boots from a national chain, the staff knowledge experience, and expertise was fantastic, and I happily parted with more cash than I'd intended on a really comfortable pair of boots.

Recently I noticed that the splits on the side of each boot were not breathable design features but a manufacturing fault. Now I'm not a big walker and I'm certainly not a hiker, local lanes, fields, hills, and the Anglesey Coastal path, hardly testing and certainly not challenging

terrain, in short, they had spent more time in the garage and certainly hadn't had anywhere near 3 years wear and tear. So, I called the store to ask for repair advice (not a replacement pair), Sam answered the phone and wasted no time in asking me 4 questions - the name of the brand, had they split on the sole (as they'd had lots of problems with this brand) had I taken out their 3-year warranty, and how long had I had them?
Answers duly received he then told me they couldn't be repaired; I'd had my monies worth and the best thing I could do is buy a new pair!

WOW pre-sale service ten out of ten, after sales service one out of ten. At which point I told him to stop digging and go and ask someone what could be done to repair them. He came back 3 minutes later and told me to bring them in so they could be looked at.

Once instore John agreed they were faulty, but he could sort things out *"so let's get your feet measured up"* but you don't have to give me a replacement pair, *"oh no you'll have to pay for a new pair"* but I just want them repaired.
Lessons 1-2: Listen and Engage

Meet Mark the store manager, his knowledge and advice was first class, he was very reassuring and gave me confidence in what he was saying. Yes, they could be repaired without damaging the waterproof inner blah blah we'd send them away to a specialist. Will that cost me anything? *"Yes of course it will"* - great a direct answer to a direct question how much? £60-£80 *"then I'm better off buying a new pair than spending that on a repair"*.

At this stage I am feeling better because I'd been heard, he'd built some rapport, given me confidence, and the knowledge to make my own decision. We agreed that I would keep the faulty boots and if my feet ever got wet, I would come in for a new pair of boots and enjoy a 20% discount off my purchase – why couldn't Sam or John done that?

Lessons 3-4: Clarity is vital and take Responsibility for the conversation. The lawn mower missed an annual service (due to covid19), and my 5-year warranty could be invalidated according to the manufacturers small print, a quick phone call to the shop I purchased it from to book it in should recover the warranty status or so I thought until I heard the price. A service was 50% of the original purchase price, when queried it the response was *"I only work here!"* Needless to say, it is being serviced elsewhere.
Lesson 5: Only employ people who reflect your company values.

After trying and failing online to find the shoes I wanted that fitted me, I went to my local shoe shop as soon as it was safe and legal to do so, to touch, feel and try on for comfort. Armed with style details, product codes, photos, and prices off their website I went to buy not browse. The shoes on my short list were either only available online or they were out of stock or not stocked at that branch and they were not allowed to transfer stock from another branch – REALLY!
"So, I'll know what size to order online, will you measure my feet please?" Oh, we don't measure feet anymore. *"Because of covid?"* No, we stopped doing it years ago. But if you go online, we have a really, good shoe size comparison guide.
Lesson 6: Give the customers what they want, not what you want.

At the checkout, the Garden Centre gift card wouldn't swipe - do you know how long you've had it? do you know how much was on it? I need to go speak to my supervisor won't be long, 5 minutes later maybe 9 or 10 minutes, with a queue behind me, people with carts full the plants and stuff, I was told they can't accept because I had to use it within 13 months of the issue date, and it expired two weeks ago – hello we've been in lockdown for months so how about 2 weeks grace. I looked behind me and decided to pay the bill and let it go … but then ask who told you that you can't accept the card – *"no one I looked it up on the computer"*.

So off I went to the Customer Service desk, I explained the situation and that the card had expired 2 weeks ago and that his colleague had looked it up on the computer and they couldn't accept it – so in front of me they looked it up on the computer and said we can't accept it. *"Can't or won't, I enquired?"*

Jayne the Manager arrives, and my experience repeated, and the same response repeated for a third time until I asked the question Can't or Won't... can't because the cards out of date and the Garden Centre would not be refunded by card supplier and won't because it's not a fair or reasonable request to justify taking money out of the till to give away.

Lesson 7: Explain the won't rather than hide behind the can't.

Back at my desk and sensing a customer experience blog in the making, I flipped the card over to get the card provider's phone number, when I noticed the card was only valid for 30 months - I'm sure they said 13 months, I'm convinced they said 13 months it certainly sounded like 13.

Lesson 8: Customers can be just as forgetful, emotional, and even stupid but then most have been out of circulation for a year or so.

> Postscript: A few weeks later I found myself in the vicinity of the Garden Centre so called in with sole purpose of apologising to Jayne, which I did along with the suggestion of asking her staff to explain the won't rather than state the can't.
> Oh, and the next time they meet a really 'stupi'" customer like me, just flip the card over and point to the 30 months.

I mentioned the retail owner's mystery shopping trip feedback above, which proved enlightening and encouraging, here's what they had to say about their High Street experiences:

> *"The service was awful. Poor displays. No masks no screens. Relied on showing me items online as they were out of stock. Didn't even ask my name. All very generic and very average. Pleasant but didn't ask any questions. Not much product information all about price and quickly discounted. Not particularly friendly but nice. Didn't try to engage".*

At the end of the trips, they left to reflect on what their customers might be experiencing in their stores and encouraged by the opportunity to differentiate themselves by offering a better experience than others.
Lesson 9: Don't assume you get it right all the time.

I've recently had the need to stay in a few hotels, one with disappointing service, one with excellent service and the others were OK, and all operated under the same strict covid19 guidelines.
After my stay at the hotel with the poor service I received an email questionnaire about my stay (note: never ask a marketer to complete a questionnaire). I kept it brief, in that it took several attempts to get the right dates on my booking confirmation despite 3 or 4 phone calls, it took a long time to check in as only one person on reception, then sent to an unmade room. The lamb at dinner was grey, thick, and tasteless, and I was disturbed four times in my room despite having paid extra for a late checkout – in the whole scheme of things nothing dramatic. I received two replies the first acknowledging my comments and a commitment to discuss them with the staff. The second informing me that it is very difficult to provide "our normal excellent service" due to the covid restrictions AND no one else had complained about their food during my stay.

The OK hotels were just that OK given the covid restrictions. BUT the excellent hotel was all down to the staff, something my colleagues commented on too! The staff were brilliant, welcoming, engaging, attentive, friendly, approachable, they took care of all our dietary needs, even the ones we'd forgotten to tell them about until they were serving us - nothing was too much trouble, they were efficient and effective. The next day I phoned the owner and told her so – she felt good, I felt good, and then we both got on with the rest of our day!
Lesson 10: Do not use Covid 19 as the excuse for poor service.

Attracting and Retaining customers isn't complicated.

-83-
12 Leadership Lessons
Forged in a Recession, Administration, a World Cup Final

At the age of 28, I was working for the John Crowther group, a clothing and carpet conglomerate which was bought for £215M by a home furnishings conglomerate called Coloroll.

Coloroll were an aggressive high growth company who would eventually spend £420M over five years on acquisitions (we were to be their largest acquisition), and their expectations and demands on us, were as high as our £215M price tag.

At the time, the UK was on the brink of a recession and by the following summer, Bank of England interest rates had hit 15%, sales of houses, home furnishings, and carpets had fallen through the floor.
Combined these factors, added an inordinate amount of pressure on the sales team to deliver the growth demands of our new owners, who had an expensive acquisition debt to finance, and for the first time I heard the phrase *"the budget is your contract"*. My job title at that time was National Account Controller, and I was responsible for sales to the major UK retailers and wholesalers.

Lesson#1: Stay calm (you can only do, what you can do).

Clearly sales growth in a recession wasn't going to be generated by doing what we'd always done, it would require something different, something impactful, something to capture the imagination, something to set us apart from the competition, and something that would significantly increase our sales, without reducing our prices.
Something like attending the biggest event on the planet - The 1990 World Cup Finals.

Lesson#2: Think outside the box (or as Steve Jobs would share sometime later Think Different).

So, I started working on the broad-brush details, contacting corporate event companies, calculating the probability of securing enough match tickets, scoping the costs, estimating the sales, and drawing out the timeline, just to see if I had something worth taking to my boss - the Sales & Marketing Director.

I had a couple of months until the following years budget was signed-off and I needed a persuasive proposition to put on his desk, if I was to secure some of his 1989 marketing budget for an event that was taking place 18 months later and wouldn't generate any additional sales for at least 9 months.

Lesson#3: Positive Realism (goes along way).

So, you can imagine the sales and marketing director's reaction when I asked a few weeks before Christmas 1988 for £156,000 for a self-funding promotion that would not only retain sales but increase sales by a million pounds, but not for another 9 months at least. With a two-tiered incentive offering a ticket to the world cup opening ceremony in Milan and a ticket to the world cup final in Rome. AND the only thing I could guarantee was the cost!

We certainly couldn't rely on any of the home country nations England, Wales, Scotland, Northern Ireland, to qualify which would reduce the appeal, but then I was (arguably) pitching an all-inclusive week's holiday with guaranteed Italian sunshine, history, culture, along with fabulous food, fine wine, beautiful cities, picturesque beaches, with no more than 3 hours of football, which just happened to be at the world cup semi-final and the world cup final at the home of the most passionate football fans on the planet!

For which there were less than 70,000 tickets for each of the games, on the entire planet, with an estimated TV audience of 26Billion – that's 5x the world's population, AND we were offering to take our best performing customers to the final. This truly was a once in a life time Golden Ticket event. And yes, my sanity was questioned.

Lesson#4: If you can't sell it internally, you'll never sell it externally.

With the numbers crunched, the forecast submitted and my reputation on the line I was given the green light by the board… and with the words *"the budget is your contract"* rattling round my head, I set about making it happen.

A Manchester events company introduced me to a Mexican company who had successfully organised the Mexico 1986 World Cup and had been appointed by the Italians to organise the Italia 90 World Cup.

As you can imagine trying to communicate in English with Mexicans and Italians was not the easiest, partly because of my lack of language skills, but more so my overriding desire for details, and guarantees – If I had a pound every time I heard the words *"don't worry" "relax" "it'll be ok" "I promise you"* I'd could have bought my own package to the final BUT their well-meant words did very little to reduce my anxiety or to inspire confidence amongst my colleagues at work. I was making regular visits to the newly inhabited South Manchester rented office in the spring of 1990, getting to know the people organising my customer trips to Italy. Then one afternoon my anxiety really spiked when I met an employee from the main global sponsor at the office, who like me was struggling with the same lack of detail and they, had committed millions.

However, these relationships would get me out of many a difficult situation over the coming months, but it was still my name on the event and my job on the line – as they say, *"your budget is your contract"*.

Lesson#5: Involve and Trust others (you can't do it alone).

On June 7th, 1990, a plane carrying company customers and hosts took off from Heathrow for Milan and the opening ceremony of the Italia 90 World Cup finals. At about the same time news began to filter through that the High Court had agreed to the appointment of Ernst & Young as receivers for the Coloroll business.

Lesson#6: Accept that stuff happens that you can't control.

If you believe in something enough, work the detail, adapt to the situation, and retain the goal.

On arrival at our head office the Administrators were not pleased to hear we had a group of staff and customers enjoying Italia '90 at their expense and instructed us to bring everyone home on the next available flight. However, once the Directors had expressed an interest in a management buyout and that the purchase value of the business would be influenced by the goodwill of our customers they were allowed to remain in Italy, as long as the bar was a pay bar. AND there was to be no further spend on the trip to the final... MY trip to the final!

I had less than 3 weeks to make it happen and with the support from 3 key suppliers and a reduced traveling party (no Directors and no Travel Rep) it was Game On – though I now had the additional roles of Host, Fixer and Tour Guide.

The night before our flight to Rome we gathered round the TV in our Heathrow hotel and watched England get through to the semi-finals of the world cup for the first time since 1966 and the dream of being in the final in a weeks' time fired our excitement.

It didn't help that I still didn't have any tickets for either match, just a large bundle of mixed group match tickets given to me by my new Mexican friends to hand over to Francesco on landing at Rome airport – whom I'd recognise by his size and sunglasses... no need to worry about missing him, he approached me within seconds of clearing customs, relieved me of my package and was gone - he was not the type of man you'd want to upset.

Lesson#7: Retain the Goal.

Our exclusive coach transfer from Rome Airport to our Naples beach front hotel didn't quite go according to plan, as we had unexpected passengers on board in the form of rowdy German fans, half the average age of my guests, high on the adrenaline and excitement of the football and the dismantling of the Berlin wall (which has started a week earlier) and all that it meant in terms of reunification of their country after 45 years under USSR control – the significance of which was not lost on some of my older guests.

3 hours later we arrived at the hotel to find ourselves locked out and security had strict instructions not to let anyone in, the hotel was full. The smoothest thing since boarding at Heathrow had been the package hand over at the airport – this was not the start I'd hoped for.

Thankfully a couple of our guests (a carpet wholesaler and his dentist friend) who had travelled out earlier to avoid Heathrow and to extend their time on the beach, alerted the manager we had arrived, and the gates were cracked open wide enough to let us through on foot, carrying our own bags.

As we finally relaxed by the pool, our Wholesaler and Dentist announced that they would be attending the England Germany semi-final straight after the Naples semi-final as they'd received an invite to visit the England team camp and were certain they'd secure tickets for the game AND would I like to join them? Their treat! Would I? Of course, I would!

The Naples Italy and Argentina semi-final atmosphere was incredible, the match was a boring 1-1 draw that took us into extra time, which threatened to play itself out for penalties. Then Argentina had a man sent off and a certain Diego Maradona playing at his Italian club's stadium decided to step up and delivered a masterclass in holding on to a result, and then scored the deciding penalty that secured their place in the final.

Lesson#8: Don't get distracted.

The night after our semi-final in Naples, England were due to play Germany in the other semi-final in Turin and our hotel had a large contingent of German fans, so I decided to secure a local restaurant with a large TV for dinner to avoid any potential flash point. Before leaving the hotel bar 3 hours before kick-off, the German fans challenged us to a bet, we eventually settled on a German win would be celebrated with Champagne, and English win with a round of beers.

We arrived in time to see coverage of the England team leaving their camp, with our two friends Fiat hire car sandwiched between the two England team coaches, with an armed police outrider escort to the ground – they'd made it!

5 hours later I returned to the hotel bar to settle our bet accompanied by one of my guests – unsurprisingly the Germans were in good voice and appreciated me honouring the bet, though not all appreciated being sprayed in champagne and being reminded of Geoff Hurst and 1966. Some responded by showering us in beer and abuse, we retreated quickly, bet settled, and a potential international incident avoided.

Lesson#9: Remember your actions set the mood.

The following day we gathered at the hotel gates and waited and waited, for our exclusive coach to arrive to take us on a morning's sightseeing tour of Pompeii and Mount Vesuvius. As the hangovers kicked-in and frustrations surfaced, it was time to put on my tour guide's hat. An hour and a half later we left on a coach organised for me by the hotel owner, at no extra cost and was ours, for as long as we wanted.

In Pompeii some of my guests returned with a Kiwi backpacker in his 20s called Miles and asked if we could give him a lift, how could I refuse I had 30 spare seats.

As we drove along the beautiful Amalfi coast road overlooking the tranquil Mediterranean Sea, a voice from the back of the coach piped up, *"Let's go to Capri"*. Being sensitive to those uncomfortable going off plan, I parented the group by setting out the rules, time frames and consequences. Yes, we could go but we must all travel back from the island on the same ferry, miss it and you find your own way back to the hotel and yes Miles could come too!

We spent a couple of hours on Capri, and all returned on the same ferry, except the coach wasn't there to meet us. Thankfully Miles was a keen middle-distance runner and leaving his belongings with us ran the 3 to 4 miles round the bay to the other port, returning the hero, riding shotgun alongside the driver on our coach.

Lesson#10: Make low cost, high value concessions.

Spirits were high and the England result forgotten as we checked back into the hotel after a full day on the road, and I collected a thicker pile of faxes than normal from reception, the essence of which, our rooms at The Imperiale Hotel on Vai Vittorio Veneto in Rome had been sold on (to the Germans) and we were to stay where we were until further notice and potentially miss the World Cup Final between Germany (2 time world cup winners) and Argentina (current world cup champions) for which I still didn't have any tickets.

My calls back to South Manchester when picked up, didn't help my situation *"stay where you are don't move, we will try to sort it out for you"*.

So, I took the decision to book enough rooms for the whole party in Rome on my personal credit card, however my personal credit limit would only cover one night - at times like this I find prayer helps!

In the morning, day 5 of our 8-day World Cup experience I gathered everyone together after breakfast and updated them on the situation.

Our hotels rooms in Rome had been double booked and we are advised to stay here.

Our hotel on the beach can accommodate us, until we fly home after the weekend.

The coach due to transfer us today has been told not to collect us, however the 'tour guide' on the coach (someone I met earlier in the week), has contacted me, and offered to pick us up if we want to continue to Rome.

I had booked rooms in Rome for the whole group but only for one night but was confident that if I could get to Rome, I could sort things out and we wouldn't be on the streets for the remaining two nights. Though this was the busiest weekend in Rome's eternal history, as everyone in the country wanted to be in the city for the World Cup Final – if only to party.

I then asked them what they wanted to do.

I watched and listened and said nothing for a few minutes – it seemed like a life time, as the room appeared to split in front of me, the men wanted to march on Rome, the women always more sensible in situations like this, quietly reminded their husbands of the benefits of staying at such a beautiful beach hotel and watching the final on TV.

Then someone suggested it was my decision, I should decide what we should do, which quickly gain traction in the room.

> *"Okay, everyone needs to be packed and in reception within the hour, we're going to Rome."*

Lesson#11: There will be times when you need to take BIG decisions.

And so, the adventure continued.

Within 20 minutes of leaving the hotel the coach driver was calling me to the front to speak to someone on his mobile phone, it sounded like Francesco the man who had relieved me of the package at Rome airport, the man you'd not want to upset. He asked me what I thought I was doing? Foolishly egged on by those on the back seat and there being 100 miles between us, I told him I knew where their office was, and we were coming to see them.

Ten minutes later they offered us a hotel on the outskirts of Rome, one joker on the back seat asked if it had a tennis court and a pool, it did not, *"did I know how many hotels in Rome had tennis courts and pools – very few"* the caller protested! *"Then we're not going there"* and I rang off.

An hour before we hit Rome, they had found rooms for us at the Ritz affectionately nicknamed the *Pitzy Ritzy* by 'our party', as there were no tennis courts and no pool, but we had rooms for the rest of our Italia '90 experience. I cancelled the other one night only hotel and gave my resuscitated credit card to my wife, along with directions to a local Taverna and hailed a taxi.

Looking at the scrawled address on a scrap of paper the driver was very uncomfortable taking a tourist to that part of town, but as they say ignorance is bliss and I insisted he took me, though I noticed once I paid the fare he did not hang around.

Just as they had taken over a residence in South Manchester, they had taken over a residence in Rome, once inside I was relieved there was no sign of Francesco and proceeded to name drop every Mexican and Italian I could remember, including Francesco. A call was made and whatever was said, resulted in me being taken to small, quiet room at the back of the apartment and introduced to a lady who I swear was Sophia Loren the Italian actress, or perhaps her twin if she ever had a twin.

The mayor's office in Rome had put Sophia into the Mexican office because *'their organised chaos'* was threatening the eternal cities' reputation.

I presented her with my pocket size itinerary booklet, detailing the names and times of the restaurants and trips we were taking, as issued months before to my qualifying guests. She explained very gently yet firmly that my itinerary was history, and she would organise a new itinerary for us.

The night before the final we ate on a private, secluded terrace in the Piazza Navona. It was a beautiful warm July evening which was only disturbed by the comings and goings of Francois Mitterrand - the French President and his entourage, and the sound of the three tenors voices coming over the terracotta rooftops from their World Cup open air concert.

The next day we went out of the city to a country club with a pool and tennis courts where we relaxed over a late pre-match lunch before our 'exclusive' coach took us to the stadium to watch the World Cup Final along with 73,000 others who had a golden ticket.

Lesson#12: Accept Help.

The Company's Italia '90 incentive ended up costing £100K not the budgeted £156K, and exceeded the budgeted £1M sales increase, by generating £1.5M in additional sales – as 'they' say *"the budget is your contract"*.

30 years on, I still get Christmas cards from some of the guests referencing THAT trip, though sadly fewer and fewer in number.

AND I have never forgotten those Leadership Lessons forged in Recession, Administration, and a World Cup Final.

-84-
Your People Notes

-85-
Your Product Notes

-86-
Your Process Notes